# GULLIVER'S TRAVELS

## Jonathan Swift

AUTHORED by Rebecca Cantor
UPDATED AND REVISED by Adam Kissel

COVER DESIGN by Table XI Partners LLC
COVER PHOTO by Olivia Verma and © 2005 GradeSaver, LLC

BOOK DESIGN by Table XI Partners LLC

Published by GradeSaver LLC, www.gradesaver.com

First published in the United States of America by GradeSaver LLC. 2007

GRADESAVER, the GradeSaver logo and the phrase "Getting you the grade since 1999" are registered trademarks of GradeSaver, LLC

ISBN 978-1-60259-107-3

Printed in the United States of America

For other products and additional information please visit
http://www.gradesaver.com

# Table of Contents

# Table of Contents

# Biography of Jonathan Swift (1667-1745)

Jonathan Swift was an author, journalist, and political activist best known for his satirical novel Gulliver's Travels and for his ironic essay on the Irish famine, "A Modest Proposal."

Born of English parents in Dublin, Ireland, Swift studied at Kilkenny Grammar School and at Trinity College in Dublin,. The abdication of King James II then drove him to England. During his time in England, Swift realized his great talent for satire and wrote *A Tale of a Tub* and *The Battle of the Books*, which were published for the first time in 1704. Swift also decided upon a career in the clergy. When he returned to Ireland, Swift became a member of the Anglican clergy, ordained in the Church of Ireland.

During the reign of Queen Anne (1702-14), Swift visited London several times, making a name for himself as a talented essayist. He began his political career as a part of the Whig political party but in 1710 switched sides, becoming a Tory and taking over the Tory journal *The Examiner*. Swift was disgusted by the Whigs' aversion to the Anglican Church and could not stand for the party's desire to do away with the Test Act, which kept many non-Anglicans from holding offices in government. Swift focused his time as a Tory on supporting their cause by writing lengthy pamphlets and essays on religion and politics, continuing to satirize those with different views. In 1713 Swift was offered the deanship of St. Patrick's Cathedral in Dublin. When Queen Anne died in 1714, the Tories came under fire, so Swift lost favor in London and greater England. He begrudgingly resigned himself to living full-time in Ireland.

In 1724 Swift led the Irish people in their resistance against the English, who continued to oppress them. He wrote many public letters and political writings with the purpose of rallying the people. One of his most famous essays, "A Modest Proposal," satirically suggests that the Irish solve their problems of starvation and over-population by eating their young. Swift also engaged in extensive commentary on religion, though these works are not much read today. Even though Swift's identity was widely known by the citizens of Dublin, no one came forward to report him when a 300-pound reward was offered for his arrest.

For the majority of his life Swift was a victim of Meniere's disease, which affects balance and hearing and causes nausea and dizziness. When Swift was about 72 years old, his disease began to keep him from his duties and social life. He became withdrawn and deeply depressed. Swift died in October of 1745. He was buried in St. Patrick's Cathedral, where he had worked as dean.

Swift was a great friend of Alexander Pope, a fellow satirist best known for "Rape of the Lock." In a letter to Pope, Swift once called himself a misanthrope, but actually it seems that he was simply frustrated by people who chose not to use the logic and reason they possessed.

# About Gulliver's Travels

Gulliver's Travels, a misanthropic satire of humanity, was written in 1726 by Jonathan Swift. Like many other authors, Swift uses the journey as the backdrop for his satire. He invents a second author, Captain Lemuel Gulliver, who narrates and speaks directly to the reader from his own experience. The original title of Swift's novel was *Travels into Several Remote Nations of the World. In Four Parts. By Lemuel Gulliver, First a Surgeon, and then a Captain of several Ships.*

Gulliver's name probably is an allusion to King Lemuel of Proverbs 31, who was a weak-minded prophet. Swift may also be connecting his character to a common mule, a half-ass, half-horse animal that is known for being stubborn and stupid. A gull is a person who is easily fooled or gullible. At the same time, Gulliver represents the everyman with his average intelligence and general good humor. The reader is able to identify with him and join him in his travels.

Even though Swift constantly alludes to events that were happening while he was alive, the story rings true today, bringing light to our own societal issues and to patterns of human nature. Throughout Gulliver's voyages, Swift goes to great lengths to scrutinize, parody, and satire various aspects of human, and often English, society. He does this in two ways, first by comparing humanity's ways with those of cultures decidedly beneath it (such as the Yahoos and the Lilliputians); second, by comparing humanity with cultures that are far superior in intellect and political ideals (such as the Houyhnhnms).

Gulliver embarks on four distinct journeys, each of which begins with a shipwreck and ends with either a daring escape or a congenial decision that it is time for Gulliver to leave. The societies Gulliver comes into contact with help him (and the reader) to examine his own culture more closely. When Gulliver's Travels was published in 1726, this examination of English culture was not appreciated. The novel was highly controversial because of the light in which it presented humanity-and more specifically, the English. When the novel was first published, Swift's identity was hidden because of the novel's volatile nature. The people who saw that the book made it into print also cut out a great deal of the most politically controversial sections, about which Swift became extremely frustrated. In a letter written under the pseudonym of Gulliver, Swift shows his annoyance with the edits made to his novel without his consent: "I hope you will be ready to own publicly," he writes, "whenever you shall be called to it, that by your great and frequent urgency you prevailed on me to publish a very loose and uncorrect account of my travels . . . . But I do not remember I gave you power to consent that anything should be omitted, and much less that anything should be inserted." The version of the novel read today is complete.

Part of what has helped Gulliver's Travels to persevere since Swift's time has been its appeal to people of all ages. The book has been read by countless children and has been made into more than one children's movie. At the same time, it has been widely critiqued and studied by literary scholars and critics, politicians, and philosophers. In addition, much like the works of Shakespeare, the comedy of the novel has something for people of all intellectual levels, from toilet humor to highbrow satires of political processes and of ideas.

# Character List

**Gulliver**

Captain Lemuel Gulliver, the narrator.

**Blefuscudians**

The sworn enemies of the Lilliputians, they live on a neighboring island. Gulliver flees to their island when the Lilliputians convict him of treason.

**Brobdingnagians**

The inhabitants of Brobdingnag. They are giant creatures relative to Gulliver.

**The Emperor**

The leader of the Lilliputians. He initially is friendly toward Gulliver but changes his mind about him when Gulliver refuses to continue fighting Blefuscu and puts out a fire in the Empress's chamber by urinating on it.

**The Farmer**

During his stay in Brobdingnag, Gulliver calls the farmer who takes him in his master. The farmer eventually sells Gulliver to the Queen.

**Flimnap**

Gulliver's enemy at Lilliput, he accuses Gulliver of sleeping with his wife.

**Glumdalclitch**

Her name means "little nurse" in Brobdingnagian. This is what Gulliver calls the farmer's daughter, who cares for him during his stay in Brobdingnag.

**Mrs. Mary Burton Gulliver**

Gulliver's wife.

**Houyhnhnms**

A species of horses who are endowed with great kindness and virtue. Gulliver lives among them for several years and afterwards is extremely reluctant to return to England.

**The King**

Gulliver and the King of Brobdingnag spend dozens of hours discussing politics and comparing their two cultures.

## Laputans

The inhabitants of a floating island who wear mathematical and astronomical symbols and have trouble paying attention.

## Lilliputians

The inhabitants of Lilliput. They are about five to six inches tall. They are the sworn enemies of the Blefuscudians of a neighboring Island.

## Munodi

The Balnibarbi Lord who shows Gulliver around and teaches him about why the island is so barren.

## Don Pedro

The captain of the Portuguese ship that picks Gulliver up after his voyage to the country of the Houyhnhnms.

## The Queen

The Queen of Brobdingnag finds Gulliver very entertaining. Because of her huge size, Gulliver is disgusted when she eats.

## Redresal

A friend of Gulliver's in Lilliput. He helps Gulliver settle into the strange new land and later helps to reduce Gulliver's possible punishment for treason from execution to having his eyes put out.

## Yahoos

The Houyhnhnms' word for humans. Yahoos in the country of the Houyhnhnms are disgusting creatures.

# Major Themes

### The Body

Throughout Gulliver's Travels the narrator spends a great deal of time discussing the human body-going so far as to detail his own urination and defecation. In each of the various lands to which Gulliver travels, he comes face to face with excrement. In Lilliput he urinates on the queen's apartment to put out a fire; in Luggnagg the professors work to turn excrement back into the food it began as; in the country of the Houyhnhnms the Yahoos throw their excrement at each other and at him.

Looking at the body from new perspectives gives Gulliver a special insight into the body's materiality. When he is relatively small, he can see the minute, ugly details of others' bodies. By looking closely at the body as a material thing and paying attention to what humans do on a daily basis, Swift makes it impossible to look at humans as exclusively spiritual or intellectual beings.

### Literature and Language

Gulliver is a reader: "My Hours of Leisure I spent in reading the best Authors ancient and modern, being always provided with a good number of books." He reads whenever he has the time. And on each of the islands he visits, he makes a point of noticing whether the inhabitants write or do not write. The Lilliputians, for instance, write diagonally like the ladies of England. The Houyhnhnms lack a form of writing, but Gulliver spends a great deal of time considering how they pass on their history.

Gulliver is also a master linguist, making him a man of virtually all peoples. On each of the islands he visits, he learns the language quickly, sometimes being taught by learned scholars (as in Lilliput) and once being taught by a young girl (in Brobdingnag). His ability to communicate suggests the value of communication across cultures. Once Gulliver has learned the language of a given society, he visits the King or Queen or Emperor or Governor and discusses politics. This ability to share knowledge is beneficial to both parties.

### Narrow-Mindedness and Enlightenment

Throughout his journeys Gulliver comes into contact with several different races of people, all of which are narrow-minded in some way. Many of the peoples are conspicuously narrow-minded, such as the Lilliputians, who have wars over the correct way to cut open an egg. (Such squabbles over unimportant matters are a common object of satire.) Even the Houyhnhnms, who are so revered by Gulliver, cannot believe there are other reasonable ways of living.

Much of Swift's satirical focus is on people who cannot see past their own ways, their own power, or their own beliefs. Readers (especially his contemporary readers) can see themselves in some of this satire.

## Otherness

Otherness plays a large part in Gulliver's Travels. Throughout his journeys Gulliver never quite fits in, regardless of how long he stays. Partly this is a matter of size. In Lilliput, he is the only giant. In Brobdingnag, everyone else is giant and he is small. Mainly, however, it is a matter of being different and simply from elsewhere. On his final journey, when he is captain and his crew mutinies, they leave him on an uncharted island. In Houyhnhnm, where there actually are human beings, they are disgusting creatures with whom Gulliver certainly cannot relate. Finally, after spending years with the Houyhnhnms and coming to consider them better in every way than humanity, Gulliver is still a human. Yet, his experience has made him an outsider in England, completely disgusted with even his own wife and children.

## Perspective and Relativity

In Gulliver's Travels the reader comes to realize that much in the world really is relative. Gulliver's first journey lands him in Lilliput where he is called the Mountain Man, because the people there are only five to six inches tall. On the other hand, in Brobdingnag, Gulliver is tiny compared to the enormous creatures who find him and keep him as a pet.

Gulliver spends a great deal of time pondering this situation when he arrives in Brobdingnag. He writes, "In this terrible Agitation of Mind I could not forbear thinking of Lilliput, whose Inhabitants looked upon me as the greatest Prodigy that ever appeared in the World: where I was able to draw an Imperial Fleet in my Hand .... I reflected what a Mortification it must prove to me to appear as inconsiderable in this Nation as one single Lilliputian would be among us." Gulliver adds, "Undoubtedly Philosophers are in the right when they tell us, that nothing is great or little otherwise than by Comparison."

Perspective and relativity do not only apply to size, however, in Gulliver's Travels. After spending time with the Houyhnhnms, Gulliver considers them above humanity in nearly every way. Returning to England, Gulliver is repulsed by the humans he formerly loved and instead chooses to spend his time in the barn with his horses. The question remains about what in the world is not relative after all; size is relative, but what about space itself? Is time relative in the novel as well? A careful reader will find many universals in the midst of so much cultural relativity.

## Travel

The novel is set in the traditional mode of satirical travel literature. Many other classic works use the same device, such as Chaucer's Canterbury Tales and Homer's Odyssey. Travel in the case of Gulliver's Travels gives Swift the opportunity to compare the ways of humanity, more specifically those of the

English, with several other ways of living. Travel also keeps the story entertaining. It is not often that a person finds a book with four sailing journeys each interrupted by torrential storms, although one should remember that the Age of Exploration in Europe provided many stories of travels and discoveries of new lands and new peoples.

## Truth and Deception

Truth and deception are prominent themes in Gulliver's Travels. For one thing, the reader is constantly questioning whether or not Gulliver is a reliable narrator-simply because what he is conveying is so fantastic. Most critics and readers determine that Gulliver is reliable, however. One sign of his honesty is established within the first few pages, when he tells the reader about where he came from.

Our comfort with Gulliver's reliability is challenged in the last chapter of the novel, though, when Gulliver tells his readers he cannot tell a lie and swears this oath: "Nec si miserum Fortuna Sinonem Finxit, vanum etiam, mendacemque improba finget," which in English means, "Nor if Fortune had molded Sinon for misery, would she also in spite mold him as false and lying."

Lying does appear within Gulliver's journeys. In Lilliput he learns that for the Lilliputians lying is a capital punishment and is considered worse than stealing. In the country of the Houyhnhnms, Gulliver is surprised to learn that the Houyhnhnms have no concept of what it means to lie. Their complete honesty is part of what makes Gulliver decide that they are the noblest creatures on Earth.

# Glossary of Terms

**abhorrence**

a feeling of repugnance or loathing

**adamantine**

hard, impervious

**ague**

a fit of shivering or shaking

**august**

impressive; eminent

**avarice**

greed

**calenture**

a tropical fever

**caprice**

an impulsive change of mind

**chimaera**

an imaginary monster

**circumspection**

being prudent

**clemency**

a merciful, kind, or lenient act

**commodious**

spacious, roomy

**coquetry**

flirtation

**declivity**

a downward slope or bend

**dexterity**

skill in using hands or body

**disapprobation**

disapproval; condemnation

**disconsolate**

heartbroken, dejected

**diuretic**

a substance used to increase excretion of urine (also used as an adjective)

**dram**

a small measurement

**ebullient**

bubbly, happy

**edict**

decree or proclamation

**edifice**

a large building

**effluvia**

a small exhalation

**encomiums**

formal tributes

**envoy**

a diplomatic agent

**equipage**

a carriage

**espalier**

a plant trained to grow in a pattern

**etymology**

the derivation of a word

**extenuation**

a partial excuse

**faction**

a dissenting clique

**hectoring**

bullying

**hermetically**

completely sealed

**hobgoblin**

a source of fear

**importunate**

troublesome, annoying

**impute**

to attribute or ascribe

**ingenuous**

artless, innocent

**laudable**

commendable

**lucid**

clear

**magnanimous**

kind, benevolent

**maliciously**

cruelly, meanly

**mercurial**

inconstant, indecisive

**misanthrope**

a hater of humankind (Swift and Pope were both consindered misanthropes)

**noxious**

toxic, harmful to living things

**odious**

bad smelling

**palisades**

a line of cliffs

**peccant**

sinful, guilty

**pecuniary**

pertaining to money

**perfidiousness**

deceitfulness or general evilness

**pernicious**

causing insidious harm or ruin

**prelate**

a high-ranking member of the clergy

**puissant**

powerful; mighty

**rapine**

plunder

**recompense**

to award compensation for

**retinue**

attendants to a high-ranking person

**rudiments**

fundamental facts or elements

**sagacity**

mental discernment, wisdom

**satire**

a literary mode in which human shortcomings are held up to scorn and ridicule

**scabbard**

a sheath for a sword or dagger

**scimitar**

a curved sword

**scrofulous**

morally tainted

**tincture**

a dye or pigment

**Tory**

a member of the conservative political party in Great Britain (1679-1832)

**usurper**

a person who takes over a position

**varlet**

an attendant or servant

**vernal**

of or pertaining to spring

**victuals**

food supplies

**virtuoso (pl. virtuosi)**

a person who is a master of his or her field

**Whig**

a member of the liberal political party in Great Britain (1679-1832)

# Short Summary

Gulliver goes on four separate voyages in *Gulliver's Travels*. Each journey is preceded by a storm. All four voyages bring new perspectives to Gulliver's life and new opportunities for satirizing the ways of England.

The first voyage is to Lilliput, where Gulliver is huge and the Lilliputians are small. At first the Lilliputians seem amiable, but the reader soon sees them for the ridiculous and petty creatures they are. Gulliver is convicted of treason for "making water" in the capital (even though he was putting out a fire and saving countless lives)--among other "crimes."

The second voyage is to Brobdingnag, a land of Giants where Gulliver seems as small as the Lilliputians were to him. Gulliver is afraid, but his keepers are surprisingly gentle. He is humiliated by the King when he is made to see the difference between how England is and how it ought to be. Gulliver realizes how revolting he must have seemed to the Lilliputians.

Gulliver's third voyage is to Laputa (and neighboring Luggnagg and Glubdugdribb). In a visit to the island of Glubdugdribb, Gulliver is able to call up the dead and discovers the deceptions of history. In Laputa, the people are over-thinkers and are ridiculous in other ways. Also, he meets the Stuldbrugs, a race endowed with immortality. Gulliver discovers that they are miserable.

His fourth voyage is to the land of the Houyhnhnms, who are horses endowed with reason. Their rational, clean, and simple society is contrasted with the filthiness and brutality of the Yahoos, beasts in human shape. Gulliver reluctantly comes to recognize their human vices. Gulliver stays with the Houyhnhnms for several years, becoming completely enamored with them to the point that he never wants to leave. When he is told that the time has come for him to leave the island, Gulliver faints from grief. Upon returning to England, Gulliver feels disgusted about other humans, including his own family.

# Summary and Analysis of Part I, "A Voyage to Lilliput," Chapters I-II

### Chapter 1

Each chapter is advertised. In this chapter, "The Author gives some Account of himself and Family, his first Inducements to travel. He is shipwrecked, and swims for his Life, gets safe on shoar in the Country of Lilliput, is made a Prisoner, and carryed up the Country."

The narrative begins with the narrator, Lemuel Gulliver, describing his childhood and the events that led him to become a seaman. He tells the reader that he is the third of five sons and that he was sent to a Puritan college at the age of fourteen. Afterwards he became an apprentice to a surgeon in London, during which time he also learned about navigation and mathematics in preparation for a future on the sea, "as I always believed it would be some time or other my fortune to do." Next he studied "Physick" (medicine) because he thought it would be "useful in long Voyages."

Afterwards Gulliver married Mrs. Mary Burton and began his life as a surgeon, taking on several patients. When his business begins to fail, he takes a six-year trip to the sea, where he serves as the surgeon to two ships and travels the East and West Indies. He spends much of his time on these voyages observing the people and learning their languages.

The real problems begin in 1699. Gulliver sets sail on a voyage that starts out prosperously but quickly takes a turn for the worse. The ship encounters violent storms, has bad food, and weakens the crew (twelve crew members die) when the ship hits a rock and is split. Six of the crew members, including Gulliver, get into a small boat and row until they are overturned by a "sudden Flurry." Gulliver swims until he is nearly exhausted, at which point he finds an island, comes across a patch of grass, and sleeps for what he estimates is more than nine hours.

When Gulliver awakens, he is lying on his back. He finds himself unable to sit up or move at all. His "Arms and Legs were strongly fastened on each side to the Ground; and [his] Hair, which was long and thick, tied down in the same manner." He feels something moving along his body almost up to his chin, at which point he sees that it is "a human Creature not six Inches high, with a Bow and Arrow in his Hands, and a Quiver at his Back." Gulliver will later learn that these creatures are called Lilliputians. Startled by this sight, Gulliver roars out and soon manages to free his left arm. The frightened Lilliputians fire dozens of tiny arrows into his hand, face, and body until he lies calmly. The Lilliputians then build a stage to Gulliver's side that is about a foot and a half tall, upon which a "Person of Quality" stands and makes a ten-minute speech to Gulliver in a language he cannot understand.

Gulliver signals that he wants food and drink, so the people bring baskets of meat and several loaves of bread, which he eats three at a time because they are so tiny to him. The Lilliputians also bring two barrels of drink, which he enjoys even though they are smaller than a half a pint together.

Gulliver admits that as he lies on the ground he often thinks of taking up fifty of the small creatures in his hand and crushing them-but he does not want to be pricked with arrows again, and he has given his "Promise of Honour" to behave in exchange for good treatment.

After he has eaten, Gulliver signals to the people to move out of the way. He relieves himself by "making Water." He promptly falls asleep because his drink had a sleeping medicine in it. Once they are sure he is asleep, the Lilliputians, who are excellent mathematicians, transport Gulliver to the Capital. They use a large platform with twenty-two wheels pulled by dozens of four-and-a-half-inch horses, dragging Gulliver half of a mile. After he awakens, Gulliver finds that he is chained by his leg in the capital, but he is able to move in a circle of about two yards in diameter. More than one hundred thousand Lilliputians come out to see Gulliver.

**Chapter II**

"The Emperor of Lilliput, attended by several of the Nobility, comes to see the Author, in his Confinement. The Emperor's Person and Habit described. Learned Men appointed to teach the Author their Language. He gains Favour by his mild Disposition. His pockets are searched, and his Sword and Pistols taken from him."

Gulliver has been allowed to move about at the end of his chain and to retire into his small house. He gives a detailed description of his need to relieve himself after two days without defecating-and how he finally does so, first in his house because of embarrassment and on every following day early in the morning so that it can be carried away by two workers before the general population is awake.

The emperor comes to visit Gulliver. The two attempt to converse even though they cannot yet understand each other's language. Gulliver tries to speak to the emperor and his men in every language he knows, but to no avail.

Gulliver is given a strong guard to protect him against those citizens who enjoy pestering him. When a group of six citizens is caught shooting arrows at Gulliver, one of which narrowly misses his left eye, they are given to Gulliver to punish as he sees fit. Gulliver puts five of the men in his pocket and dangles the sixth above his mouth as if he is going to eat him, but he then lets all of the men go, gaining favor with those who are watching.

During this time the emperor holds many conferences with his wisest men, trying to decide what to do with Gulliver. They are worried that he could escape or that he could cause a famine because of how much food it takes to keep him satisfied. It is eventually decided that two officers should be appointed to search Gulliver with his assistance. Afterwards, Gulliver is asked to demonstrate the purpose of each of the items found on his person. When he fires his pistol into the air, several of the Lilliputians fall to the ground in fright.

Analysis

Gulliver begins the story of his journeys in the typical pattern of the travel narratives of his time. He tells the reader a great deal of background information, such as where he was born, which schools he attended, and his profession. The reader learns that Gulliver began his life in a very usual way. He was basically middle-class and had to work for a living. By setting up the narrator as a normal person in the beginning of the book, Swift helps readers to sense that Gulliver is trustworthy and a regular guy whom they can relate to. While a more fantastic narrator may have been more impressive and exciting, for the satire to work best, readers are placed in Gulliver's everyman shoes.

The perception that Gulliver is trustworthy diminishes, however, as soon as Gulliver comes into contact with the Lilliputians. It is obvious that the creatures are figments of Swift's imagination, since it is extremely unlikely that such beings actually exist. But Gulliver's trustworthiness is unimportant insofar as the reader recognizes that the real conversation is with Swift. We continue happily on Gulliver's journey in order to find out what Swift wants us to perceive through the tale.

At the time that Swift wrote Gulliver's Travels, England was the most powerful nation in the world, with a large fleet of ships, which were constantly searching for new lands to control. During these searches the English came into contact with several new civilizations. The Lilliputians seem almost possible in this context. But Swift chooses to set the first culture Gulliver comes into contact with as far too small to be real. He makes the Lilliputians only six inches tall. It is significant that Gulliver, coming from the most powerful nation in the world, is able to be held prisoner by six-inch men. Swift is asking the English to consider the pride of their own country, especially as a colonial power. A great number of small people can overpower one large person-if they are resourceful enough. Are England's colonies powerful and crafty enough to do it?

At the same time, it is apparent that even though Gulliver fears the tiny arrows of the Lilliputians, he could almost certainly escape if he put his mind to it. Why does he choose to stay? Perhaps he is curious about the Lilliputians, their culture, language, and ways of living. Gulliver's curiosity and thirst for knowledge were established in the first few paragraphs of the novel. Or perhaps Gulliver enjoys the power that comes with being a giant. Even as a prisoner in Lilliput, Gulliver is the most powerful being on the island.

# Summary and Analysis of Part I, Chapters III-IV

### Chapter III

"The Author diverts the Emperor and his Nobility of both Sexes in a very uncommon manner. The Diversions of the Court of Lilliput described. The Author hath his Liberty granted him upon certain Conditions."

Because Gulliver has been behaving so well, the emperor, his court, and the general population are beginning to trust him. Gulliver also has made a great deal of progress in learning the language and learning about the culture he is now such a large part of.

The emperor decides to entertain Gulliver by showing him a tradition of the court in which candidates for an open position of honor compete by walking to the middle of a string or tight-rope that is suspended two-and-a-half feet above the ground. They jump as high as they are able. "Whoever jumps the highest without falling succeeds in the Office." Gulliver tells the reader that very often these competitors are injured or fall to their death.

Gulliver's hat is found washed upon the shore, and he asks the emperor to command his men to bring it to him. It is worn from being dragged the half-mile to the kingdom, but it looks tolerably good. The emperor then asks Gulliver to stand up tall with his legs spread apart so that his troops can march through them.

Gulliver is finally granted his freedom on the condition that he (1) swear to help the Lilliputians if they are ever in a war, (2) survey the surrounding land, (3) help with any building that needs to be done, and (4) deliver messages. He agrees. In return he will be granted the food and drink sufficient for 1,724 Lilliputians.

### Chapter IV

"Mildendo, the Metropolis of Lilliput, described, together with the Emperor's Palace. A Conversation between the Author and a Principal Secretary, concerning the Affairs of that Empire: The Author Offers to serve the Emperor in his Wars."

The first thing Gulliver wants to do once he is free is see the metropolis of Lilliput. He finds the town very impressive. It is "capable of holding five hundred thousand Souls" and has two great streets that are five feet wide and cross in the middle, quartering the city. At the center is the emperor's palace. When Gulliver reaches the palace, the empress reaches her hand out the window for Gulliver to kiss.

Two weeks later Redresal, the Principal Secretary of private Affairs, comes to see Gulliver and tells him about the "two mighty Evils" that Lilliput struggles against: "a violent Faction at home, and the Danger of an Invasion by a most potent Enemy from abroad." He describes two parties of Lilliput, the Tramecksan and Slamecksan, who are distinguished by the high and low heels of their shoes. The emperor has decided to permit only low heels in the administration of Lilliput.

Redresal and the Lilliputians also have to worry about the threat of invasion from those living on the Island of Blefuscu, "which is the other great Empire of the Universe." The people of Lilliput and Blefuscu are unable to get along because years ago, after an emperor's son was injured trying to break his egg on the smaller end (the traditional way of egg breaking), he decreed that no one may break the smaller end of his egg. This caused a great uproar among many of the Lilliputians and led to six rebellions and thousands of deaths. Eventually the Big-Endians were exiled and went to Blefuscu, where they gained favor and convinced the government to go to war against Lilliput.

Gulliver finishes the conversation by telling Redresal that, while he does not want to interfere, he is "ready, with the hazard of [his] Life, to defend his Person and State against all Invaders."

Analysis

These two chapters highlight the kinds of commentary Swift makes throughout the novel. By describing a society that chooses its highest officials with silly competitions like seeing who can jump the highest on a tight-rope, Swift is poking fun at the way officials are chosen in England. He is also commenting on the disturbing trend of politicians who are willing to do whatever it takes to gain favor in the court-including humiliating themselves. The danger of ambition is also figured here; jumping badly can lead to death.

Having Gulliver stand with his legs apart so that the Lilliputian armies can walk through is also a ridiculous idea. It is a comment on the pomp and circumstance of English armies. To Swift it seems that armies are often more concerned with looking impressive than with being impressive. This scene might also be an allusion to the Colossus of Rhodes, described in Julius Caesar by Shakespeare as a larger-than-life figure that men could walk through the legs of.

The contract Gulliver signs in order to gain his freedom further highlights the unequal relationship between Gulliver and the Lilliputians, but it is a relationship where a cordial contract trumps simple power. Gulliver could easily take control and break the contract, but he chooses to be peaceful.

The war between the English and the French is parodied in the conflict between the Lilliputians and the Blefuscudians. Their conflict over which end of the egg to break reflects the centuries-old conflict over how to practice religion-as Protestants or Catholics. While the wars over religion certainly were very serious, Swift suggests that what was being fought over (at least on the religious rather than the political side) really was not very important. In Swift's eyes, fighting over religion is as pointless as fighting over which end of an egg to break.

Swift also parodies the political parties within England. The Tory party is represented by the Low Heels while the Whigs are represented by the High Heels. Considering that Swift himself changed parties, he must have understood that political allegiance was important. Yet, political bickering is often about such unimportant matters as the height of one's heels.

# Summary and Analysis of Part I, Chapters V-VIII

**Chapter V**

"The Author by an extraordinary Stratagem prevents an Invasion. A high Title of Honour is conferred upon him. Embassadors arrive from the Emperor of Blefuscu, and sue for Peace. The Empress's Apartment on fire by an Accident; the Author instrumental in saving the rest of the Palace."

When the Lilliputians and Blefuscudians go to war, Gulliver proves to be very useful by dragging the entire Blefuscudian fleet of ships to the shore of Lilliput, where "The Emperor and his whole Court stood on the Shore expecting the Issue of the great Adventure." When Gulliver arrives, he cries out, "Long live the most puissant Emperor of Lilliput!" The emperor gives Gulliver the land's highest honor, "Nardac."

Later the emperor requests that Gulliver go back to the enemy's shores and do his best to destroy what is left, turning the empire into a province. Gulliver thinks that this action is going too far and declines the request. Three weeks after Gulliver's victory, an embassy from Blefuscu arrives offering peace, which the emperor accepts.

A few days later Gulliver is awoken at midnight by hundreds of Lilliputians telling him that there is a fire in the empress's chamber in the palace. Gulliver hurries to be of assistance, but he quickly realizes that the thimble-sized buckets he is being passed are not having an affect on the raging fire. Thinking quickly, Gulliver chooses to urinate on the fire, putting it out completely and keeping it from spreading to the rest of the palace.

Gulliver returns to his home, where he awaits word of how the emperor and empress will react to his deed. He shortly learns that the empress feels abhorred.

**Chapter VI**

"Of the Inhabitants of Lilliput; their Learning, Laws and Customs, the Manner of Educating their Children. The Author's way of living in that Country. His Vindication of a great Lady."

Gulliver goes into great detail about what he has learned about the Lilliputians, their customs, and their culture. He tells the reader that everything in Lilliput is proportionate to the Lilliputians' size and that even their eyesight is adjusted so that they can see things closer than Gulliver can.

Gulliver also describes many of Lilliput's laws, telling the reader that dishonesty and false accusations are punished more severely than theft and other terrible things are punished in England. If someone in Lilliput accuses another but is proven to be wrong in the accusation, the accused is punished severely while the falsely accused person is rewarded.

Also, Gulliver tells the reader that children are raised by the state rather than their parents. Different classes learn about different things. The nobility's children, for instance, learn about honor, justice, courage, modesty, clemency, religion, and love of country.

Gulliver ends the chapter by straightening out a falsehood created by Flimnap, who has "always been [his] secret enemy." Gulliver declares that Flimnap's accusation that Gulliver carried on with his wife is completely untrue, which should reestablish the lady's reputation.

**Chapter VII**

"The Author being informed of a Design to accuse him of High-Treason, makes his escape to Blefuscu. His Reception there."

A high member of the court arrives to tell Gulliver that he is being charged with treason. Originally his sentence was to be death, but Redresal has argued successfully to have the sentence lessened to the removal of Gulliver's eyes. The charges Gulliver has been accused of are "making water" in the royal palace, refusing to reduce Blefuscu to a province, aiding the ambassadors of Blefuscu when they came to ask for peace, and planning to visit Blefuscu.

Not wanting to have his eyes put out, Gulliver flees to Blefuscu, where he is warmly received.

**Chapter VIII**

"The Author by a lucky Accident, finds means to leave Blefuscu; and, after some Difficulties, returns safe to his Native Country."

While in Blefuscu, Gulliver spies a ship that is the proper size for him to sail in. He spends about a month making repairs, during which time the emperor of Lilliput sends a message demanding that Gulliver be returned so that his sentence can be carried out. The emperor of Blefuscu sends back a message refusing. Gulliver eventually sets sail and is picked up by a merchant ship and returned to his home, where he makes a solid profit showing Lilliputian-sized livestock he has carried home in his pockets.

Analysis

The contract for Gulliver's freedom proves pointless. He promised in writing to serve the emperor, which he does by capturing the enemy's fleet. But when the emperor asks him to go back and destroy the enemy, Gulliver refuses-and there is nothing the Lilliputians can do to persuade him. The contract, in this case, is completely useless. Power proves more important, and it is fortunate that Gulliver uses his reason to decide how to use his power appropriately. (Again one might consider the implications for England as a colonial power.)

When Gulliver puts out the palace's fire by urinating on it, Swift is doing more than making a joke that one should pee on the problems of the state. A fire is a serious thing. One serious implication is that royalty is ephemeral. The royal palace can catch on fire just like anything else, and when it does, no amount of royal power can put it out, just physics-and the dirty side of nature at that. Gulliver proves the point when everyone under the emperor's power is trying to put out the fire with their tiny buckets, and he realizes the only way to put it out is by urinating. Swift is also showing the reader something about the ridiculous needs of royalty, because even though Gulliver has saved the palace he has done so in a blameworthy manner.

Most of the time in Gulliver's Travels when Gulliver tells the details of a society's ways of living, Swift is satirizing something wrong with English society. This can occur when he describes the society negatively, but it also can occur by demonstrating a difference between the other culture and his own. It is apparent that many of the Lilliputian customs are attractive to Swift. For instance, in Lilliput, lying is a capital offence. We see this again when we meet the Houyhnhnms, the noblest race on Gulliver's journey, who do not understand the concept of saying that which is not true. Swift suggests that lying is worse than several of the blameworthy offences in England.

It is interesting to note that even though lying is seen as a terrible offense in Lilliput, Flimnap tells a huge lie (that Gulliver slept with Flimnap's wife) and gets away with it. Apart from the ludicrous physical implications of a giant having relations with a Lilliputian, the problem here is that the society must be able to enforce its norm against lying for the law to matter. This may also be a commentary on the seeming ability of those in positions of power to get away with breaking the law. When the law comes down unfairly on Gulliver, he has actual rather than statutory power to leave, so he simply leaves Lilliput to live with their enemies.

# Summary and Analysis of Part II, "A Voyage to Brobdingnag"

### Chapter I

"A great Storm described, the long Boat sent to fetch Water, the Author goes with it to discover the Country. He is left on Shoar, is seized by one of the Natives, and carry'd to a Farmer's House. His Reception there, with several Accidents that happen'd there. A Description of the Inhabitants."

On June 20, 1702, ten months after his return from Lilliput and Blefuscu, Gulliver returns to the sea in a ship named *Adventure*. The journey begins very smoothly, the only delay being caused by an illness contracted by the captain. They continue on their journey for several months until a storm begins to brew, pushing the *Adventure* several miles off track. On June 16, 1703, the crew sees land and drops anchor, at which point the captain sends a dozen men on shore to fetch water. Gulliver wanders away from the other men to observe the countryside until he sees them in the boat hurrying back to the ship. He tries to call out to them, but he sees that they are being chased by a giant-though the giant is not able to catch the boat. Gulliver runs as fast as he can into the island.

Gulliver finds that much of the island is well cultivated, but to his surprise, when he comes across a hayfield, he realizes that the grass is more than twenty feet tall. Similarly, corn is at least forty feet high. Gulliver sees another giant, this time well-dressed, walking along the path he is on. He notes that each of the giant's strides is about ten yards long. The well-dressed giant is joined by seven workers, whom he instructs to begin reaping the corn (though Gulliver cannot understand the language).

Exhausted and filled with despair, Gulliver lies down and hopes that he will die. He writes, "I bemoaned my desolate Widow, and Fatherless Children." He begins to think back on the Lilliputians who thought that he was such a powerful and strong creature, saying that he now feels as a single Lilliputian would feel among humans. "Undoubtably," he muses, "Philosophers are in the right when they tell us, that nothing is great or little otherwise than by Comparison."

When he is about to be stepped on by one of the farmers, Gulliver cries out as loudly as he can. The giant stops short and picks up Gulliver to get a better look. Gulliver resists struggling in order to avoid being dropped sixty feet to the ground and instead brings his hands to a prayer position and points his eyes skyward. The giant seems pleased with Gulliver and, putting him in his pocket, heads over to show his master.

The master takes Gulliver home to show his wife, who screams at first, but when she sees how polite Gulliver is, she quickly warms up to him. Gulliver and the farmer try to speak to each other but are unsuccessful. At dinnertime, Gulliver sees that the full family consists of the parents, three children, and an elderly grandmother. The farmer's wife breaks up some bread and a small piece of meat and hands them to Gulliver, who gets out his knife and fork and proceeds to eat, thoroughly delighting the whole family. Later, as Gulliver walks across the table toward the farmer (whom he now calls his master), the farmer's son picks him up by one leg and dangles him in the air until the farmer grabs him back and boxes the boy's ear. Gulliver, not wanting to make an enemy in his new home, signals that he would like the boy to be pardoned, which he is.

At this point an infant is brought into the room, who at the sight of Gulliver cries to get him into its hand-with which the mother obliges. Quickly the baby squeezes Gulliver and puts his head in its mouth, at which Gulliver cries out until the baby drops him, luckily into the mother's apron. The baby cannot be quieted until the nurse nurses it. The sight of the woman's breast is repulsive to Gulliver. It is so large in his view that he can see all of its defects.

After dinner Gulliver signals that he is tired. The farmer's wife sets him on her bed and covers him with a handkerchief, where he sleeps until two rats the size of large dogs startle him. Gulliver fights them with his hanger (a short sword), killing one and scaring the other away.

Afterwards Gulliver signals that he needs time alone in the garden to relieve himself. He asks the reader to excuse him for dwelling on particulars.

## Chapter II

"A Description of the Farmer's Daughter. The Author carried to a Market-Town, and then to the Metropolis. The Particulars of his Journey."

Gulliver is given into the care of the farmer's daughter, Glumdalclitch, who teaches him the language and treats him very well, like a child would care for a favorite doll. In fact, she keeps him in a doll's cradle, which she closes inside a drawer at night to keep him safe from the rats.

As word of Gulliver spreads throughout the kingdom, the farmer begins to realize that there is profit to be made and takes Gulliver to the marketplace, where he performs shows for paying patrons. The show is so successful that the farmer decides to take Gulliver on a tour of the kingdom. Gulliver does ten shows a day, which makes him quite tired.

## Chapter III

"The Author sent for to Court. The Queen buys him of his Master the Farmer, and presents him to the King. He disputes with his Majesty's great Scholars. An Apartment at Court provided for the Author. He is in high Favour with the Queen. He stands up for the Honour of his own Country. His Quarrels with the Queen's Dwarf."

Having heard about the wondrous little creature that is making his way around the kingdom, the queen sends for him and his master to come to court. Gulliver immediately impresses the queen with his compliments and general manner, so she asks the farmer if he would be willing to sell Gulliver. The farmer, believing that Gulliver will die in about a month because he has lost so much weight from performing, quickly names a price. Gulliver is happy to live at court and be done with performing. He asks only that Glumdalclitch stay as well to continue taking care of him.

Afterward the queen carries Gulliver to the king's chamber. The king at first believes that Gulliver is some sort of mechanical creature, but he eventually believes that Gulliver is just helpless. Gulliver tries to explain that where he is from, everything is proportionate to him.

The queen has a small apartment built and new fine clothes tailored for Gulliver. She enjoys his company very much. Gulliver often comments that watching the Brobdingnag people eat or getting too close to their faces is quite repulsive.

Gulliver and the king spend a great deal of time discussing politics. Gulliver explains how things work where he is from. The king laughs at English politics, which puts Gulliver off at first. Soon, however, Gulliver realizes that his adventures have begun to sway him to the same opinion; his perspective has begun to change.

Gulliver finds an enemy in the queen's dwarf, who seems to be jealous of all the attention Gulliver is getting.

## Chapter IV

"The Country described. A Proposal for correcting modern Maps. The King's Palace, and some Account of the Metropolis. The Author's way of travelling. The chief Temple described."

Gulliver spends a great deal of time describing the landscape of Brobdingnag, the palace that he now lives in and his manner of traveling in a small traveling box designed especially for him. He also sees and describes the largest temple in Brobdingnag, which he does not find impressive in its size.

## Chapter V

"Several Adventures that happened to the Author. The Execution of a Criminal. The Author shews his Skill in Navigation."

Serving in Brobdingnag proves difficult for Gulliver. He experiences a series of dangers because of his small size-and because the dwarf relishes in making Gulliver's life difficult. The ladies at court treat Gulliver like a toy, dressing and undressing him and undressing themselves in front of him. Gulliver again mentions how offensive he finds the skin and smell of the Brobdingnagians. He remembers the Lilliputians' similar reaction to his smell, which he did not understand at the time. Gulliver nearly drowns when a toad jumps onto the boat the queen has had made for him. He is also carried to the top of the palace by a monkey and narrowly survives. The monkey is killed, and it is declared that monkeys will no longer be allowed in the palace.

## Chapter VI

"Several Contrivances of the Author to please the King and Queen. He shews his Skill in Musick. The King enquires into the State of Europe, which the Author relates to him. The King's Observations thereon."

Gulliver salvages several of the king's hairs from his shaving cream and makes himself a comb. He then makes the seat of a chair from the queen's hair but refuses to sit on it because doing so would be insulting to her. He also makes Glumdalclitch a small purse.

Gulliver spends the evening at a concert in Brobdingnag. For him the music is so loud that he cannot enjoy it unless his traveling box is brought as far away as possible and all of the windows and doors are closed.

Gulliver often goes to see the king, who requests a detailed description of the government of England, which Gulliver relates. The king asks him many questions, challenging various aspects of the government and having particular difficulty with England's violent past. In the end the king concludes that the English are well below the Brobdingnagians, calling them "the most pernicious Race of Little odious Vermin that Nature ever suffered to crawl upon the Surface of the Earth."

## Chapter VII

"The Author's Love of his Country. He makes a Proposal of much Advantage to the King, which is rejected. The King's great Ignorance in Politicks. The Learning of that Country very imperfect and confined. Their Laws, and military Affairs, and Parties in the State."

Gulliver is offended by the manner in which the king has dismissed the English as a lowly society. He tries to impress the king by telling him about some of the many great inventions of England, beginning with gunpowder. Gulliver goes into great detail about the power and effect of gunpowder and what the king could accomplish with it, saying that he could easily control everyone in Brobdingnag with gunpowder. The king is "struck with Horror" and disgusted by Gulliver's proposals. He tells Gulliver that if he values his life, he should never mention gunpowder again. Gulliver cannot believe that the king would reject such an immense opportunity. Gulliver then discusses the general ignorance of the Brobdingnag people, including their simple laws and practices.

# Chapter VIII

"The King and Queen make a Progress to the Frontiers. The Author attends them. The manner in which he leaves the Country very particularly related. He returns to England."

Gulliver has been in Brobdingnag for two years and strongly feels that it is time to leave. He is basically being treated as a pet. But the royal family does not want to part with him. Coincidentally, on a trip to the seashore, a giant eagle picks up Gulliver's traveling box and flies off with him. Realizing that the box is not edible, the eagle drops it into the sea. After some time the box is picked up by a passing ship of Gulliver's normal proportions. Gulliver finds it very difficult to adjust to the size of things back in England. He feels much larger than the others.

Analysis

Whatever Gulliver did not gain in perspective (in terms of size) during his time in Lilliput, he gains in Brobdingnag. His time here not only gives Gulliver an understanding of what it is like to be powerless, but it also shows Gulliver how the Lilliputians must have felt when near him. Of course this situation is even more intimidating because here there are many giants, while in Lilliput he was the only one. This is how a Lilliputian would feel in England. The differences Gulliver experiences between the two islands are heightened because of the close proximity of the trips. Gulliver feels even smaller in Brobdingnag than he would have felt if he had never journeyed to Lilliput.

Gulliver's newfound understanding of perspective helps him to feel powerless more profoundly-first for himself, when he curls up and rather pathetically hopes to die, and then for others, especially for the Lilliputians he left behind. As his fear rises, he becomes more and more emotional, eventually becoming so overwhelmed that he gives up, curling up into the fetal position.

Once Gulliver is brought to the farmer's house, many challenges await him because of his lack of power in this land. A mere baby threatens his life, as do two common rats. Gulliver is able to fight them off in a seemingly heroic fashion, but it is clear that he could have lost the fight. Gulliver is also surprised by the aesthetic differences of the world from this new perspective. The nurse's breast is disgusting to him because he can clearly see every deformity and blemish. He imagines what the Lilliputians thought of his physicality.

In these chapters we again see Gulliver as less than heroic. Just as in Lilliput, when Gulliver did not fight against his captivity (as Odysseus might), here Gulliver does nothing to try to avoid being captured. He waits until he is about to be stepped on before taking any action at all. And he only begs for mercy from the giant Brobdingnags. Gulliver relies on the protection of a young girl who tucks him into a doll's cradle at night. Gulliver survives and thrives only partly on the basis of his good manners. For the most part, he is a pet and a curiosity.

Gulliver's compliance continues when he is required to perform so that the farmer can earn money. Gulliver becomes drastically emaciated, but he never resists what he is being told to do. In fact, readers do not really learn that Gulliver hated his task until he is out of danger and complains to the queen of Brobdingnag. Once Gulliver is seemingly safe at the court and has gained favor with the queen, he remains a plaything with very little respect, especially from the ladies at court.

As a tiny person in the Brobdingnag world, Gulliver endures several trials that a larger person would never have to suffer. This again reminds the reader of the importance of physical strength as well as intellectual strength. Even when combat is not an issue, a large stature intimidates one's opponent. As a tiny person, Gulliver is left to the whims of those around him. In the fifth chapter, for instance, Gulliver is captured by a small monkey that would have been a minor threat in England.

The overreaction of the queen and the rest of the government to this incident sheds important light on the Brobdingnag government. It seems that this government is rash. The killing of the monkey also shows that Gulliver has more status in the court than that of a toy or an animal. His nemesis is the dwarf, who used to be the small man in court.

The king and Gulliver have long conversations about politics, but the king never really considers Gulliver's opinions on important matters. Being small, Gulliver is considered petty, and the idea of gaining power through gunpowder is anathema to the king. Through Gulliver's discussions with the king, the reader learns that perspective extends beyond size to opinion. After several days of discussing the governments of England and Brobdingnag, the king declares the English to be "the most pernicious Race of Little odious Vermin that Nature ever suffered to crawl upon the Surface of the Earth." Again Gulliver's Travels brings light to the fact that people from different backgrounds often have different opinions on the same subjects, even though people tend to follow similar patterns. Gulliver finds that each people prefers its own ways, but a traveler who spends a long time elsewhere might (or might not) come to prefer the foreigners' ways over his own. Experience, thought, and tradition are important considerations in making this choice.

As for gunpowder, for Gulliver (and through him, the English), gunpowder represents the height of achievement primarily because of the power it has provided. The Brobdingnag king, however, is not corrupted by power. He is able to see that the negative effects of gunpowder would far outweigh the positive ones in his society. He might be right that Gulliver is narrow-minded, but his tirade on the general stupidity of the Brobdingnags takes the opposite point of view. Still, on this issue he is unable to see his own faults or those of his society. It is up to Swift to show us, through Gulliver's tale, what Gulliver's insistence on gunpowder means.

# Summary and Analysis of Part III, "A Voyage to Laputa ... and Japan"

### Chapter I

"The Author sets out on his Third Voyage, is taken by Pyrates. The Malice of a Dutch-man. His arrival at an Island. He is received into Laputa."

After being at home for only ten days, Gulliver is visited by a ship captain who invites him on a voyage departing in two months. Gulliver convinces his wife that this is a good opportunity and sets off, again working as the surgeon.

After they sail for three days, a storm arises, driving the ship to the north-northeast, where they are attacked by pirates. They are unable to defend themselves. Gulliver insults the captain of the pirate ship and as punishment is set adrift in "a small Canoe, with Paddles and a Sail, and four Days Provisions."

On the fifth day of sailing in his canoe, Gulliver reaches a small island, where he spends the night in restless sleep. In the morning he notices that what he thought was a cloud floating above the island is actually a floating island. Gulliver calls up to the people he sees moving about the island. They lower down a system of pulleys that can pull Gulliver up.

### Chapter II

"The Humours and Dispositions of the Laputians described. An account of their Learning. Of the King and his Court. The Author's Reception there. The Inhabitants subject to Fears and Disquietudes. An Account of the Women."

As soon as Gulliver steps onto the floating island, he is surrounded by a crowd of people. He finds them very strange even though they are of a size similar to his. Their heads are slanted to the left or right, and their clothes have pictures of either musical instruments or astronomical signs.

Gulliver learns that he is on Laputa. The people here have terribly short attention spans, so they carry around "Flappers." These are used for hitting other people during conversation in order to keep them focused. After dinner a man is sent to teach Gulliver the language.

Gulliver finds that the Laputian houses are built very poorly and with no right angles. This is odd because the men here are obsessed with mathematics. The people here never have peace of mind. They are constantly worrying about dangers such as the possibility that the sun might go out. The women are very sexual creatures who often cheat on their husbands, especially with their preferred men from Balnibarbi, but the men are so wrapped up in mathematics that they do not notice. The King of Laputa is not remotely interested in the government of England.

## Chapter III

"A Phenomenon solved by modern Philosophy and Astronomy. The Laputians' great Improvements in the latter. The King's method of suppressing Insurrections."

Gulliver learns that Laputa is floating above Balnibarbi, the island on which he landed his canoe. Laputa contains 10,000 acres and is perfectly circular. It is able to move about the surface of Balnibarbi but not beyond its borders, and it can move up and down because of its magnetic forces. When a town from Balnibarbi acts up, the King has Laputa moved directly above it so that it can receive no sun or rain. No one from the Royal family is allowed to leave Laputa.

## Chapter IV

"The Author leaves Laputa; is conveyed to Balnibarbi; arrives at the Metropolis. A Description of the Metropolis, and the Country adjoining. The Author hospitably received by a great Lord. His Conversation with that Lord."

Gulliver finds Laputa terribly boring because the people there are all much more intelligent than he is. He has a hard time conversing with them and is generally ignored. He petitions to go down to Balnibarbi, and his request is granted. On Balnibarbi, Gulliver meets Lord Munodi, who invites Gulliver to stay at his home. Munodi's home is beautiful and kept well, but when the two travel out into the country Gulliver finds that the rest of the land is barren and sadly kept. Munodi explains that this is because many years back, people from Balnibarbi visited Laputa, and when they returned they decided to change things to a more academic way of living. This idea has failed. Munodi's land is plentiful because he never changed his way of living.

## Chapter V

"The Author permitted to see the grand Academy of Lagado. The Academy largely described. The Arts wherein the Professors employ themselves."

Gulliver visits the Grand Academy of Lagado, the largest metropolis of Balnibarbi. The scientists there are constantly working on experiments that Gulliver finds pointless. For instance, he meets a man who is trying to extract sunlight from cucumbers. Other experiments are trying to turn excrement back into the food it began as, trying to make gunpowder from ice, and trying to employ spiders as weavers of silk. Professors are also attempting to alter the communication of Balnibarbi by doing away with language altogether.

## Chapter VI

"A further account of the Academy. The Author proposes some Improvements, which are honourably received."

Gulliver then visits the part of the Academy designated for studies of government. He finds the professors especially in this wing to be entirely crazy. They propose such things as studying excrement to find treasonous people and taxing people based on beauty and wit.

## Chapter VII

"The Author leaves Lagado, arrives at Maldonada. No ship ready. He takes a short Voyage to Glubbdubdrib. His Reception by the Governor."

Gulliver decides to take a trip to the Island of Luggnagg but finds that no ships will be available for the voyage for a month, so it is suggested that he visit Glubbdubdrib, which he translates to mean the island of sorcerers or magicians. Once he arrives in the governor's home, he finds that "The Governor and his Family are served and attended by Domesticks of a kind somewhat unusual." Gulliver learns that the governor has the power to bring back the dead for the purpose of serving him. Gulliver is given the option to bring back anyone he would like. He chooses Alexander the Great, who tells Gulliver that he actually died because he drank too much. He then brings back a parade of other famous dead.

## Chapter VIII

"A further Account of Glubbdubdrib. Antient and Modern History corrected."

Gulliver spends a great deal of time speaking with various famous dead people. He speaks with Homer, Aristotle, and Descartes and even gets them into conversation with one another. He later brings back a few English Yeomen and finds them much larger and stronger than the English people today. He worries that his countrymen are diminishing with time.

## Chapter IX

"The Author's Return to Maldonada. Sails to the Kingdom of Luggnagg. The Author confined. He is sent for to Court. The manner of his Admittance. The King's great Lenity to his Subjects."

Gulliver travels to Luggnagg, posing as a Dutchman. He says, "I thought it necessary to disguise my Country, and call my self an Hollander, because my Intentions were for Japan, and I knew the Dutch were the only Europeans permitted to enter into that Kingdom." His true identity is discovered, however, and Gulliver is made a prisoner. He later learns that anyone who wants to come before the king must crawl on hands and knees and lick the floor. The king, it turns out, uses this tradition to his advantage when he wants to get rid of someone-simply by poisoning the floor.

## Chapter X

"The Luggnaggians commended. A particular Description of the Struldbrugs, with many Conversations between the Author and some eminent Persons upon that subject."

Gulliver learns about the Struldbrug children who are born to Luggnaggians but who have a red dot on each of their foreheads. These children are immortal, which causes Gulliver to fantasize about what he would do if he were immortal. He dreams of the ability to take his time becoming a master of many different subjects and amassing great wealth. But Gulliver soon comes to learn that the Struldbrug children are actually very unhappy and jealous of those people who can die. They find their own lives depressing.

## Chapter XI

"The Author leaves Luggnagg and sails to Japan. From thence he returns in a Dutch Ship to Amsterdam, and from Amsterdam to England."

After offering Gulliver employment in the court but finally seeing that he is determined to leave, His Majesty gives him license to leave, a letter of recommendation to the Emperor of Japan, and a gift of 444 pieces of gold and a very valuable red diamond. In Japan he is told to trample the crucifix, which all Dutchmen are happy to do, but Gulliver manages to get out of doing so. He takes a ship to Amsterdam and then to England, where he happily returns to his family.

Analysis

Again, Gulliver arrives at his new adventure in dramatic style, this time being cast from his ship by pirates and left to drift about the sea. The time alone serves as a kind of existential preparation for encountering a new society. He arrives exhausted, hungry, thirsty and alone, completely ready to take in new ideas and opinions. Even so, he finds many of the Laputians' ideas difficult to swallow. In general, Part III gives Swift a chance to try out a number of ideas for alternative civilizations, and each one could support its own full narrative.

On Laputa, the floating island, Swift creates a way of physically stratifying a society. Those who work with their hands for a living-and the ridiculous professors-live on Balnibarbi. The upper class, including the royal family and the more able intellectuals, live on the floating island of Laputa. In this way Swift makes the separation between the two types of people visually obvious, with the better above the lesser.

We also learn that when a town from Balnibarbi acts up and needs to be punished Laputa is moved above them, blocking out the sun and rain. This signifies a serious problem that Swift sees in many governments. Justice should only be about retribution when necessary, but the royalty makes the citizens even more unhappy by taking away that which they need to live. Swift indicates that rebellions could be avoided all together if the citizens' satisfaction became a priority of the royalty.

One main difference between the people of Laputa and the people of Balnibarbi is that those living in Laputa have very limited attention spans. One thinks here of the absentminded professor.

Indeed much of what goes on there seems to be related to the curse of being smart but impractical. Although the people of Laputa are very intelligent, it gets them little. With their slanting heads, they do not see things directly as they are. They seem to have no common sense, which for someone like Swift, who cares a great deal about the material world, may be more important than raw intelligence. Because of their lack of sense, they spend too much time worrying about ridiculous things rather than noticing what is really wrong in their own lives. They are so unaware that the men do not know that their wives cheat on them. This emasculating fact is all too common for the unmanly intellectual.

When Gulliver visits Balnibarbi, he finds that the people have suffered an even worse fate. Being unsuited for the intellectual life, they have tried to live on the basis of pseudo-academic life and have failed miserably. The land has become barren because the people neglect it completely. Instead they focus all of their attention on their ridiculous academics. By trying to be something they are not-that is, like many would-be intellectuals-the Balnibarbi people have lost what they once had, and now they are left with nothing. Swifts comments here on the importance of self-evaluation and living the life to which one is suited. There is elitism here, with the lower people needing to understand their natural place-but it is an elitism based on nature. A society needs many different kinds of people in order to survive, and not everyone should be an intellectual-and besides, the intellectuals do not do so well themselves.

In Glubbdubdrib, Gulliver is able to bring back great figures from history, including truly wise people such as Aristotle. Nearly everything that he learns is different from what has been recorded in the history books. Swift shows here that history cannot be trusted, especially because those involved typically are not the ones who write their own history. The trouble now is that Swift has shown us that we cannot trust others and we do not often do well when we falsely trust in ourselves. We must trust in ourselves but only with a clear view of who we really are-our proper location, perspective, and size all matter.

In Luggnagg, Gulliver meets a king who has his courtiers lick the floor as they approach him, crawling on their hands and knees. Once again, we find Swift commenting on the ridiculous rules of royals who abuse their power.

Immortality turns out not to be as wonderful as many people think. The Struldbrugs are depressed, perhaps because there is no reason to act quickly. They have all the time in the world. Meanwhile, they have plenty of time to see what mortals have done for themselves and their society in their fleeting time alive.

It is interesting that Swift includes Japan, a real place, among these fantastic places. In his time, Japan was a closed society that did not generally want to traffic with the outside world. It was at the far edge of the East and as mysterious as these truly fictional places.

# Summary and Analysis of Part IV, "A Voyage to the Country of the Houyhnhnms," Chapters I-VI

### Chapter I

"The Author sets out as Captain of a Ship. His Men conspire against him, confine him a long Time to his Cabin, and set him on Shoar in an unknown Land. He travels up into the Country. The Yahoos, a strange Sort of Animal, described. The Author meets two Houyhnhnms."

After five months at home, Gulliver leaves his children and pregnant wife yet again to go on his fourth voyage, this time as captain. Not long into the trip, his crew mutinies, locking him into his cabin for a great deal of time and threatening to murder him. Eventually the crew, who plan to become pirates, drop Gulliver off on an unknown island.

Gulliver walks inland until he comes across a field of strange creatures. After observing them for some time he comments, "Upon the whole, I never beheld in all my Travels so disagreeable an Animal, nor one against which I naturally conceived so strong an Antipathy." Soon Gulliver comes to realize that these are actually naked human beings behaving like cattle. Gulliver comes face to face with one of them. He hits it with the side of his blade when it comes at him violently. The animal-like human (which Gulliver later learns is called a Yahoo) cries out, causing the rest of the forty Yahoos to surround Gulliver.

Gulliver fears the worst until the Yahoos suddenly flee because of a grey horse coming toward them. The horse takes an interest in Gulliver and circles him until another horse comes along. Gulliver observes that their whinnies to each other sound almost like a language. Gulliver hears the word Yahoo several times and repeats it to the great surprise of both horses. The horses then teach Gulliver the word Houyhnhnm, which Gulliver later learns is their word for themselves-for horse. Afterward, the grey horse signals to Gulliver that he should walk in front of him, which he does.

### Chapter II

"The Author conducted by a Houyhnhnm to his House. The House described. The Author's reception. The Food of the Houyhnhnms. The Author in Distress for want of Meat. Is at last relieved. His Manner of feeding in this Country."

Gulliver and the grey horse arrive at a home where Gulliver expects to meet the horse's human masters. The two move through every room of the house and meet several other horses before Gulliver realizes that the grey horse is the master of the house.

After some discussion between the horse and his wife about whether or not Gulliver is in fact a Yahoo, he is brought out to the stable where the Yahoos are kept and is made to stand next to one of them. Aside from the extra hair, longer nails, and nakedness of the Yahoo, they are the same.

Gulliver makes a kind of bread out of the horses' oats for his dinner and is given a small room near the house with some hay to sleep in.

## Chapter III

"The Author studies to learn the Language. The Houyhnhnm his master assists in teaching him. The Language described. Several Houyhnhnms of Quality come out of Curiosity to see the Author. He gives his Master a short Account of his Voyage."

After about three months of living among the Houyhnhnms, Gulliver has learned their language quite well and can answer most of their questions. He tells them about the mutiny that landed him on their shores, but they have a very difficult time understanding, because they have no concept of what a lie is. They tell Gulliver that "The Word Houyhnhnm, in their Tongue, signifies a Horse, and its Etymology, the Perfection of Nature."

The horses believe that Gulliver is a Yahoo-but a more rational and civilized Yahoo. Gulliver, wanting to separate himself from the Yahoos as much as possible, asks not to be called a Yahoo anymore.

## Chapter IV

"The Houyhnhnms' Notion of Truth and Falsehood. The Author's Discourse disapproved by his Master. The Author gives a more particular Account of himself, and the Accidents of his Voyage."

Gulliver continues explaining the concept of lying to his master. He also explains the relationship of horses and humans back in England. The horses cannot believe that humans would be able to control creatures that are so much stronger than they are, but Gulliver explains that horses are tamed beginning at a very young age.

## Chapter V

"The Author at his Master's Commands informs him of the State of England. The Causes of War among the Princes of Europe. The Author begins to explain the English Constitution."

Over the next two years, Gulliver explains much about the English government and political systems. Gulliver tries to explain war and the reasons why humans kill each other. His master says that Yahoos in England are worse than Yahoos because they use their reason to gain power but use it badly.

## Chapter VI

"A Continuation of the State of England. The Character of a first Minister."

Gulliver continues telling his master about the vices of the English people. He paints a particularly disturbing picture of lawyers and doctors, saying that lawyers are the stupidest among the Yahoos and doctors are corrupt and seldom cure their patients.

Analysis

In the country of the Houyhnhnms, Gulliver meets the species that is the most skeptical of him-and for good reason. Gulliver must do everything he can to separate himself from the Yahoos, a very different situation from his distinct positions in Lilliput and Brobdingnag. In order to accomplish this, Gulliver does small things daily like using his best manners, eating with a knife and fork, keeping his clothes on, and being as clean as possible. He shows that he can use language, can reason well, and can be prudent and mannerly.

It is interesting to note that from the very beginning of his time in the country of the Houyhnhnms, Gulliver strives to separate himself from his own species. Is this what Swift has been trying to do his entire life? It often is difficult to strive for individual human greatness among a mass of people who hardly try and have hardly any notion of what greatness would be. In Brobdingnag, when Gulliver explained the English people and their way of life to the king, the king decided they were lowly creatures and Gulliver became offended, trying to defend his people. Something is different now in the country of the Houyhnhnms. When the grey mare tells Gulliver that he thinks his people are worse than the Yahoos, Gulliver is quick to agree.

What is different here? Only Gulliver's experiences since Brobdingnag and his contact with the Yahoos. Through the Yahoos, Gulliver has come to see some awful aspects of human nature, and Swift has shown his readers what they would be (and often are) without the intelligence and graces of which they are capable. Gulliver seems willing to turn his back on the English people in favor of those he deems better than the English. Now that he has been exposed to many alternatives, he can think carefully about who to admire and what political systems to favor, and the English certainly come up short in relation to the Houyhnhnms.

Also interesting in these chapters is Gulliver's plain admonishment of lawyers and doctors. Gulliver's negative commentary about lawyers is in many ways not surprising except for its level of ferocity. Lawyers seem no better than politicians, going to court over the petty human squabbles that Gulliver satirized as early as Part I. Gulliver's description of doctors as shallow and greedy people who would kill a patient as soon as cure him is surprising to contemporary readers, especially because

Gulliver has spent so many years working as a surgeon. One should remember that eighteenth-century medicine was still rather poor.

# Summary and Analysis of Part IV, Chapters VII-XII

## Chapter VII

"The Author's great Love of his Native Country. His Master's Observations upon the Constitution and Administration of England, as described by the Author, with parallel Cases and Comparisons. His Master's Observations upon Human Nature."

Gulliver has come to love the Houyhnhnms, their society, and their way of living. He writes, "I had not been a Year in this Country, before I contracted such a Love and Veneration for the Inhabitants, that I entered on a firm resolution never to return to human Kind, but to pass the rest of my Life among these admirable Houyhnhnms in the Contemplation and practice of every Virtue."

Gulliver then describes a conversation with his Master in which he is honored by being asked to sit farther away. His Master tells Gulliver that his conclusion, after learning all about Gulliver's fellow human beings, is that they are not as different from Yahoos, "their Brethren," as originally thought.

## Chapter VIII

"The Author relates several Particulars of the Yahoos. The great Virtues of the Houyhnhnms. The Education and Exercise of their Youth. Their general Assembly."

In order to study the Yahoos more closely, Gulliver asks to spend some time among them, which is granted. Gulliver is completely disgusted by the Yahoos. They smell terrible, are completely unkempt, and act ridiculously, even throwing their excrement at one another. When Gulliver sneaks away to a pond for a bath, he is nearly assaulted by one of the female Yahoos but is saved by a Houyhnhnm.

## Chapter IX

"A grand Debate at the General Assembly of the Houyhnhnms, and how it was determined. The Learning of the Houyhnhnms. Their Buildings. Their manner of Burials. The Defectiveness of their Language."

Gulliver's master attends a great assembly as the representative of his district. When he returns he tells Gulliver that they were discussing whether or not to exterminate the Yahoos-and that he suggested they be castrated when young, just as Gulliver told him horses in England often are. That way they will be easier to tame, and they will eventually die off. In the meantime, the Houyhnhnms can breed asses, which are much stronger and more manageable than Yahoos.

Gulliver tells the reader that the horses have no system of letters and do not read or write, but that they maintain their knowledge through oral tradition. They also have very few diseases and can calculate the year by the revolutions of the sun. Houyhnhnms live to about seventy or seventy-five years old, and when they die no one makes a big fuss.

## Chapter X

"The Author's Oeconomy and happy Life among the Houyhnhnms. His great improvement in Virtue, by conversing with them. Their Conversations. The Author has notice given him by his Master that he must depart from the Country. He falls into a Swoon for Grief, but submits. He contrives and finishes a Canoo, by the help of a Fellow-Servant, and puts to Sea at a venture."

Gulliver is given a nice room in the Houyhnhnms' home, where he settles in very comfortably. He makes new clothes and enjoys his life very much. The other Houyhnhnms, however, begin to worry about a Yahoo living among Houyhnhnms. They fear that Gulliver may lead a revolt among the other Yahoos. They tell Gulliver's master that it is time for him to leave the island. When Gulliver hears this news, he faints from grief. Having no other choice, Gulliver builds a canoe over the next two months. Heartbroken, he sets sail, but not before kissing his master's hoof.

## Chapter XI

The Author's dangerous Voyage. He arrives at New-Holland, hoping to settle there. Is wounded with an Arrow by one of the Natives. Is seized and carried by Force into a Portugueze Ship. The great Civilities of the Captain. The Author arrives at England."

Gulliver paddles away from the shore, determined not to go too far from the Houyhnhnms. He writes, "My Design was, if possible, to discover some small island uninhabited, yet sufficient by my Labour to furnish me with the Necessaries of Life, which I would have thought a greater Happiness than to be first Minister in the Politest Court of Europe." He finds a small island, where he lives for four days on raw oysters and other shellfish until he is discovered by the natives. He runs to his canoe and rows away, but not before being shot in his left knee.

Gulliver sees a Portuguese ship, but he feels disgusted by the thought of sharing a ship with Yahoos, so he chooses to return to another side of the same island. The Portuguese land and find Gulliver. He refuses to leave, but the crewmates decide not to leave him by himself on the island. The captain, Don Pedro, is very kind to Gulliver, but Gulliver cannot stand to be near Yahoos, so he spends most of the voyage in his cabin alone.

Finally back in England, Gulliver's family is thrilled to see him alive, but Gulliver thinks of them only as Yahoos and cannot stand to be near them. He buys two horses and spends at least four hours a day in the stables conversing with them.

## Chapter XII

"The Author's Veracity. His Design in publishing this Work. His Censure of those Travellers who swerve from the Truth. The Author clears himself from any sinister Ends in writing. An Objection answered. The Method of planting Colonies. His Native Country commended. The Right of the Crown to those Countries described by the Author is justified. The Difficulty of conquering them. The Author takes his last leave of the Reader; proposes his Manner of Living for the future; gives good Advice, and concludes."

Gulliver concludes the tale of his travels, saying that everything he has written is true. He also tells the reader that he is now able to eat at the same table with his family although he is still working to teach them to overcome their vices. He only wants to help the world he lives in to become more like the world of the Houyhnhnms.

Analysis

Gulliver tells his master about the way horses are treated in England, and the master cannot believe it, just as the English would never believe that there was a place where humans are ruled by horses. Yet, in the country of the Houyhnhnms, this relationship makes perfect sense. (Compare Planet of the Apes.) Again perspective plays an important role in Gulliver's journeys. There has been a major change between the two places. Here the horses have intelligence and virtue while humans, according to the grey mare, are different from Yahoos only in appearance-their morality is the same. Gulliver does not disagree. Swift encourages us to consider what really does distinguish better and worse examples of humanity.

Swift creates an interesting parallel between the governments of the Houyhnhnms and of the English when the grey horse attends the great assembly-both exhibit similar senses of entitlement to rule on the basis of merit. The Houyhnhnms are discussing whether or not to exterminate the Yahoos, never pausing to discuss whether or not they have the right to subjugate and kill the morally weaker species. Similarly, the English colonists of Swift's time often felt moral superiority to the native peoples-but if they really were like Yahoos, they had little right to think so. And even if they were superior in various ways, the English needed to think carefully about the alternative ways of ordering life and society before deciding what to do about it-as Gulliver has learned.

The Houyhnhnms' decision to do away with the Yahoos is very interesting. First of all, the idea to slowly kill off the race by castrating the males came from Gulliver. He has directly contributed to the destruction of a subspecies of his own race, but he shows no remorse. Also, the horses seem to feel better about killing off the Yahoos slowly by keeping them from breeding rather than actually murdering them, even though the end result is the same.

Even though the reader has been on Gulliver's side throughout his adventures so far, here we wonder if Gulliver has gone too far in giving up on humanity in favor of another species altogether. Why would he choose to abandon his people, his life, and his family? It is true that Gulliver is the kind of person who is called to the sea, to live apart from traditional society. And we understand the criticism of humanity, especially if we have some of the religious sensibilities of most of Swift's readers, knowing that humans are flawed in many ways. Can we redeem ourselves? When Gulliver returns, he slips into his reclusive state, spending large amounts of time talking to his horses, but he retains some interest in helping humans become better-apparently through the work of comparing alternatives and choosing what is better-the life of the Houyhnhnms.

Meanwhile, one should not forget that even though the Yahoos are disgusting, they express something attractive about human nature. The Yahoos have strong emotions and are sexual beings. They have fun, frolicking and playing in the fields. They are not afraid to get dirty or to have less-than-perfect manners. The Houyhnhnms, on the other hand, do not have love, do not shed a tear when one of them dies, and are aloof and rather cold. Perhaps it is not so bad being a Yahoo-but we should be wary of this pull toward rough-and-tumble life. It was not quite right to be an absentminded intellectual, and it is not quite right to be aloof like the Houyhnhnms, yet it is not quite right to be a Yahoo. We must consider the alternatives and decide for ourselves.

# Suggested Essay Questions

1. Consider Gulliver's stated intentions in writing about his travels. What do the letters at the beginning of the work reveal about his character? What kind of a person is Gulliver? Why is he driven to the sea repeatedly even as his wife and children wait at home?

   Answer: Gulliver repeatedly heeds the call to go off to sea. He claims that it is for commercial reasons, but Gulliver easily adapts to foreign cultures and usually does not mind seeing how another culture might be superior to his own. He is a reader and a traveler, not the kind of person who feels bound to traditional society.

2. Perspective and relativity are very important aspects of Gulliver's Travels. Compare Gulliver's experiences in the first and second parts of the novel. How does Gulliver act differently? How is he treated differently?

   Answer: In the first part, Gulliver is the giant; in the second, everyone else is a giant. In both, he is the outsider and is treated as such. Consider the power relationships in each part and the ability of prudence and reason to overcome differences in perspective.

3. Bodily functions are described often and in great detail in the novel. Why is Swift so graphic?

   Answer: Humanity's base functions comprise an important aspect of the novel? Swift pays great attention to the real world, the material world where people actually have to live their lives. In addition to the slapstick value of associating different things in the text with excrement, Swift reminds us that we are embodied mortals.

4. Is Gulliver a hero?

   Answer: One may choose to compare Gulliver's actions and characteristics with other great characters such as Odysseus, who also has great sea adventures, or Jason and the Argonauts. Odysseus is crafty and strong, but Gulliver does not endure great hardships or overcome great enemies. This is a satire, not an epic, so we neither expect nor need a hero. Instead, Swift gives us a narrator who tells his own story as an everyman. The point is that he is not greatly different from an average human being, though he becomes much wiser and more thoughtful.

5. Is Gulliver a reliable narrator?

   Answer: We generally trust his statements even though they are about fantastic beings and places. We do not need to believe that such things actually happened. Instead we should recall that Swift has important lessons to teach though the satire and the imaginary narrator of these fictional travels. Beyond that, we might trust Gulliver because of his thoughtfulness and prudence in some ways and because he is willing to relate good news and bad news, good and bad things about various kinds of people, in the same even tone.

6. Discuss Swift's connection to Gulliver.

Answer: The author need not share the narrator's opinions, but we always should keep in mind that it is Swift who has presented a narrator with certain opinions. Sometimes, Swift's joke is at Gulliver's expense. Also consider Gulliver's attack on humanity in Part IV.

7. What makes the Houyhnhnms' society ideal or a model for humans?

Answer: From Gulliver's perspective, the Houyhnhnms have established the ideal society. In fact, when he returns home to England, he cannot stand the sight or smell of humans and prefers to spend his time in the barn with his horses. The Houyhnhnms are more rational than the Yahoos and the other peoples in the novel. Note other ways that the Yahoos are unlike the Houyhnhnms.

8. How does Gulliver change as the novel progresses? For instance, at the end of the novel, when Gulliver is spending time in the barn with his horses, do we as readers identify with him, or are we repulsed?

Answer: Gulliver learns much about alternative ways of living and comes to appreciate the ways that various peoples have improved upon the ways that he knew in England. He also appreciates what it is like to be much larger or smaller, much better or worse, much more practical or less intelligent, than others. He has seen how what is an important difference within a culture seems petty to outsiders. Overall, he sees many things more objectively and has come to despise the usual ways of humans where he lives. The horses are not really like the Houyhnhnms, so we realize Gulliver's mistake, but we sense that Gulliver is better off with a lot of time to himself to contemplate his experiences and what they mean for living well.

9. Compare the satire in this novel with the argument in Swift's short essay, "A Modest Proposal," in which he declares that the Irish should eat their children in order to keep from starving.

Answer: "A Modest Proposal" purports to solve a number of problems with a simple but morally impossible solution. One's outrage at the proposed solution should be channeled into thinking about a real solution--including the moral elements of the solution. The novel takes on society and subgroups, and the ways we live, more than any particular problem, showing us more about human nature. This difference is in large measure a reflection of what can be done in an essay versus a novel.

10. Who is Swift making fun of and why?

Answer: A good answer will examine ways in which human nature as a whole is satirized as well as ways that the British are satirized and the ways that particular groups (such as intellectuals) are satirized. In each case, find something ironic or humorous, determine at whose expense we laugh, and decide why we are laughing. Sometimes we laugh because our intentions have unintended consequences, sometimes we are inconsistent or irrational, and sometimes we laugh when we see ourselves as outsiders would see us.

# Important Quotations

"Thus, Gentle Reader, I have given thee a faithful History of my Travels for Sixteen Years, and above seven months, wherein I have not been so studious of Ornament as Truth. I could perhaps like others have astonished thee with strange improbable Tales; but I rather chose to relate plain Matter of Fact in the simplest Manner and Style, because my principal design was to inform, and not amuse thee."

The Brobdingnagian king's opinion of the English: "But, by what I have gathered from your own Relation, and the Answers I have with much Pains wringed and extorted from you, I cannot but conclude that Bulk of your Natives, to be the most pernicious Race of Little odious Vermin that Nature ever suffered to crawl upon the Surface of the Earth."

"In this terrible Agitation of Mind I could not forbear thinking of Lilliput, whose Inhabitants looked upon me as the greatest Prodigy that ever appeared in the World: where I was able to draw an Imperial Fleet in my Hand .... I reflected what a Mortification it must prove to me to appear as inconsiderable in this Nation as one single Lilliputian would be among us .... Undoubtedly Philosophers are in the right when they tell us, that nothing is great or little otherwise than by Comparison."

"But, as my sole Intention was for the PUBLICK GOOD, I cannot be altogether dissapointed. For who can read of the Virtues I have mentioned in the Glorious Houyhnhnms, without being ashamed of his own Vices, when he consideres himself as the reasoning, governing Animal of his Country? I shall say nothing of those remote nations where Yahoos preside ... But I forbear descanting further, and rather leave the Judicious Reader to his own Remarks and Applications."

# Author of ClassicNote and Sources

Rebecca Cantor, author of ClassicNote. Completed on June 29, 2007, copyright held by GradeSaver.

Updated and revised Adam Kissel August 21, 2007. Copyright held by GradeSaver.

DeGategno, Paul J. Critical Companion to Jonathan Swift: A Literary Reference to His Life and Works. New York: Facts on File, 2006.

Fox, Christopher, ed. The Cambridge Companion to Jonathan Swift. Cambridge: Cambridge University Press, 2006.

Hammond, Brean, and Shaun Regan. Making the Novel: Fiction and Society in Britain, 1660-1789. Basingstoke: Palgrave Macmillan, 2006.

Swift, Jonathan. Gulliver's Travels. Ed. Albert J. Rivero. New York: Norton, 2002.

Clegg, Jeanne. "Swift on False Witness." Studies in English Literature, 1500-1900 44:3 (Summer 2004), pp. 461 ff.

Rabb, Melinda. "The Secret Memoirs of Lemuel Gulliver: Satire, Secrecy, and Swift." ELH 73:2 (Summer 2006), pp. 325 ff.

# Essay: The Child-like Scientist: A Study of the Similarities Between Jonathan Swifts' Gulliver's Travels and Voltaire's Candide in Reference to Satire Developed through Naivete

**by Arthur-Damon Jones**
**June 01, 1999**

A child has the ability to make the most critical and objective observation on society and the behavior of man. How is this possible? A child has yet to mature and lacks proper education and experience. However, it is for this very reason that a child would make the perfect social scientist; his or her naivete may provide an excellent means of objective criticism and most often satire. A child's curious nature and hunger for knowledge would bring about an unbiased questioning of social structures, minus the brainwashing of these very institutions, and his or her vulnerability would expose any societal dangers present. This child-like scientist would see the truth as it is.

This same premise may be applied to literary works. A naive character or narrator may be used as a child-like scientist, who reveals social truths to the audience through his or her naivete. As Maurois has noted, in writing about Candide, by Voltaire," It was novel of apprenticeship, that is, the shaping of an adolescent's ideas by rude

contact with the universe" (101). Jonathan Swift also takes this approach in his work Gulliver's Travels, where Gulliver, the main character, provides a naive point of reference.

The satires Gulliver's Travels, by Jonathan Swift, and Candide, by Voltaire, both make use of naivete to convey satirical attacks on society. In both works, litotes [understatements] are made of extremely absurd situations, which further illuminates the ridiculous nature of a situation. Characters in each novel are made vulnerable by their overly trusting natures. This is taken advantage of, and these characters are left exploited by corrupt people in society. Attacks are also made on authority figures of the world. This can be seen in the characters' reaction to authority. Finally, both works are travel tales, which expose the main characters to many perspectives. This allows the authors to satirize many aspects of society.

These two satirical works make litotes of preposterous situations, thus shedding light on the absurdity at hand. This is an especially effective technique, because a character or narrator is involved in a ridiculous situation. The reader, from an aesthetic distance, is then able to recognize the foolishness of the incident. After careful consideration, a satirical conclusion may be drawn. For example, Voltaire's narrator describes a brutal battle scene in a lighthearted manner:

> Nothing could have been more splendid, brilliant, smart or orderly than the two armies . . . . then rifle fire removed from our best of worlds about nine or ten thousand scoundrels who had been infesting its surface. The bayonet was also the sufficient reason for the death of several thousand men. (22-23)

The diction in this passage is ironic. By referring to a battle as "splendid" (22) and "brilliant" (22), the narrator demonstrates how common the idea of warfare has become and how little the human life is valued. Also, the phrase, "Our best of worlds" (22-23) identifies optimism as a focus of this satirical attack (Maurois 100). In this way, the narrator nonchalantly discusses grave matters. Maurois cited both Voltaire and Swift as using this method when he states, "and from the Dean [Swift] he [Voltaire] had learned how to tell an absurd story in the most natural manner" (104). In this way, the foolish scenarios stand out in the context of "serious" discourse, and when taken in on a satirical level, the narrator's carefree consideration of dreadful events suggests a desensitizing of society.

Quintana, in his essay "Situation as a Satirical Method," describes Swifts' satire as a "situational satire." In this method a situation is created and objectively observed in order to produce satirical attacks (344-346). This method is the same as the one described earlier. The audience, once having stepped back from the dramatic situation, realizes the absurdity of it, and the satirical point being made. When speaking with the King of Brobdingnag, Gulliver describes many absurd characteristics of human life in Europe, which to Gulliver, seem noble. He especially treats gunpowder with litotes (Bk. I, ch. 6-7). The lofty manner in which Gulliver presents his culture ironically accents the ignoble qualities of Europe.

Another example may be drawn form Gulliver's stay in Lilliput. In attending the "political" ceremonies of Lilliput, Gulliver takes serious consideration of the ridiculous system of gaining political favor and power. Politicians perform "rope dances" in order to gain political rank. (Bk. I, ch. 3). Here Gulliver's being gullible is used as a political attack on the superficiality if politics. In both works, characters or narrators make understatements or treat absurd subjects with complete sincerity, thus creating a situation from which satirical observations may be drawn.

Another way in which naivete is used in these two tales is to satirize the tendency of corrupt people to take advantage of overly trusting individuals. Both Gulliver and Candide fit the description of the overly trusting, naive character. Van Doren chronicles this situation as demonstrated in Gulliver's Travels:

> Grateful for the kindness shown on him, Gulliver aided the Lilliput in this war by capturing the Blefuscudian fleet and bringing it as a gift to his royal host. But the Lilliputians were no more grateful

than the English had been to the Oxford ministry for ending the
war with France. . . . The sourest of the tiny ministers became
Gulliver's enemy. (187)

Here Gulliver too easily places his trust in the hands of strangers. This naive move
leaves open the opportunity for the Lilliputians to betray him. Swift is able to
satirically attack human's behavior through this "situational irony" (Quintana
344-346). In this particular situation, Swift demonstrates how dangerous being
overly trusting may be. Gulliver believes that he has made friends in the Lilliputians.
However, by the end of the visit he is almost executed (Bk. I). On a satirical level,
Swift asserts that the corruptive human being is deadly when overly trusted.

The dangers of being overly trusting are also discussed in Candide. In chapter 19,
Candide is taken advantage of by a conniving captain. Candide, who has just
acquired great wealth from El Dorado, is overcharged for passage on a ship. Then he
entrusts his possessions with the captain, who flees with Candide's riches (ch. 19).
Here Voltaire rejects an "optimistic" (Maurois 100) approach to philosophy. The
audience realizes that Candide has been swindled out of his belongings by confiding
in a "trustworthy" citizen of the "best of all possible worlds" (Maurois 100). Again
naivete is used to create satire, in this case, an individual's overly trusting nature is
wrongly taken advantage of and results in a loss of property or even a near death
experience.

Another aspect of society that is attacked in both of these novels is authority figures.
In each case, Gulliver or Candide's reactions to authority are used as satirical
devices. In the case of Candide, positive progress is made after a period of naive
subordination. In Gulliver's case, the hierarchical structures of society keep him in
constant submission.

Candide at first blindly accepts his teacher's highly optimistic philosophy. It takes
Candide a while to begin to question this authority. Voltaire contends that authority
figures should be questioned and their doctrine should not be taken at face value.
Voltaire's negative tone towards Candide's naive following of Pangloss' optimism is
seen at aesthetic distance in the context of devastation after devastation that occurs.
Pangloss' philosophy is obviously not holding up. This leads Candide to an
evaluation of this authority. Pasco describes this intellectual growth that occurs after
the questioning: when Candide says early in chapter 13 that had Pangloss lived,
Candide would have dared to object to the master's continual insistence that all is for
the best in the best of all possible worlds, we know something has taken place. This
is the first of several indications that Candide has begun a process of development
that will leave him considerably less naive. (94) Candide is able to become less naive
and thus less subordinate.

The same is unfortunately not true for Gulliver. He has been conditioned by a
hierarchical society to internalize his submissive role. This internalization is apparent
when he first encounters the Lilliputians, Gulliver states," I answered in a few words,

but in the most submissive manner" (36). The audience is to consider the drastic size difference between Gulliver and the Lilliputians. It is absurd for Gulliver the bow down to these microscopic islanders. Once this has been assessed, Swift's satirical attack on hierarchical structures is made clear; certain institutions foster a socially stratified culture, of which Gulliver is a product. Again his submissive nature emerges in his contact with the Houyhnhms. Lawler mentions Gulliver's position with the Houyhnhms when he notes, "the final realization that even as a servant and disciple there can be no place for him [Gulliver] in the land Houyhnhms" (323). In this land Gulliver readily takes his submissive role, as a result of his experience with hierarchical authority. In both novels, different satirical points are made about authority, but they are both done through the same medium of a naive character's reaction to authority.

Finally, both works may be regarded as travel tales, which expose the naive characters to various perspectives. This allows the authors to satirize various aspects of human nature and universalizes the satire. Clark further describes Gulliver's role:

> Indeed it was never long before he [Gulliver] comprehended the inhabitants of the lands he chanced upon. In this respect he was a typical voyager. (2)

In the "Introduction to Gulliver's Travels" this sentiment is also expressed. The author states that," Swift adopts an ancient satirical device: the imaginary voyage" (905). Gulliver travels to far and unknown lands, and is presented with new perspectives that satirize lands very familiar to the reader. The world seen through his naive eyes can be interpreted as Swift's satire. Van Doren comments on the affect of these various perspectives, using Brobdingnag as an example:

> But after the giant, he [Gulliver] could not so easily return to the old scale. . . his own people seemed contemptible by their smallness. (189)

And again by using Houyhnhm as an example: "The reasonable Houyhnhms said he had noticed the rudiments of all these human ways of life among the yahoos" (193). These alternate perspectives provide revelations for Gulliver about his society and human nature in general. As the naive traveler is enlightened, the reader recognizes the satirical significance of the situation (Quintana 344-346).

Mylne similarly classifies Candide when she states, "Tories like Zadig and Candide were in the tradition of the voyage imaginaire and the Oriental travel-tale" (216). Candide's journey spans across many nations and both hemispheres. He is exposed to different philosophies and people. This allows the author to satirize different aspects of society. Candide is especially given a new perspective at El Dorado. In El Dorado, gold is treated like dirt. There is little value that these citizens place on material possessions. This episode acts as a satirical attack on the materialism of the world. In tune with the message of the final chapter, "we must cultivate our garden" (123),

Bottiglia divides the many settings of the novel into gardens. He states that:

> Westphalia is the center of optimistic fatalism   Bulgares is a
> naked military despotism, while Paraguay is a military despotism
> masquerading as a kingdom of God on earth. Holland is a
> mercantile utopia . . . Lisbon is the home of Inquisitory fanaticism .
> . . Orellions is the habitat of state-of-nature savagery . . .[El
> Dorado] offers a philosophic ideal for human aspiration. (91)

Here the scholar provides an extensive example of the many perspectives present and the ideals that are satirized. In each arena Candide's experiences and interaction with others are the breeding ground for Voltaire's satire. In both Candide and Gulliver's Travels this universal satire is made possible by the stories' being travel-tales in which the protagonists are exposed to many different lands and perspectives.

As can be seen, child-like naivete can be a helpful tool in criticizing or satirizing a subject. When an amateur approaches a subject ignorant of the topic, his or her mistakes may be learning experiences for those observing. That is exactly the case with these two novels. As stated in the "Introduction to Gulliver's Travels"," Through Gulliver's eyes, we gaze on marvel after marvel" (906), and through these naive characters' experiences and satires are developed. Understatements are made of absurd incidents. This reveals the preposterous nature of the situation. The naive characters place too much trust in the hands of strangers. This vulnerability allows for the exploitative nature of humans to be exhibited. These characters' reactions to authority act as a medium to satirize authority figures and hierarchical structures. Finally, the travel aspect of these stories creates many perspectives from which universal topics of satire may be drawn. In this manner, naivete reveals truths about human nature.

**Works Cited**

<ul>

<li>Bottiglia, William F. "Candide's Garden." Voltaire A Collection of Essays. Ed. Bottiglia, William F. Englewood Cliffs: Prentice Hall Inc., 1968.

<li>Clark, Paul O. A Gulliver's Dictionary. New York: Haskell Publishers, 1972.

<li>Green, F. C. French Novelist Manners and Ideas. New York: D Appleton and Company, 1929.

<li>"Introduction to Gulliver's Travels." Norton Anthology of English Literature, The Major Authors. Ed. M.H. Abrhams et al. Sixth ed. New York: W. W. Norton and Company, 1995.

<li>Lawler, John. "The Evolution of Gulliver's Character." Norton Critical Editions.

<li>Maurois, Andre'. Voltaire. New York: D. Appleton and Company, 1932.

<li>Mylne, Vivienne. The Eighteenth-Century French Novel. Manchester: University of Manchester Press, 1965.

<li>Pasco, Allan H. Novel Configurations A Study of French Fiction. Birmingham: Summa Publications, 1987.

<li>Quintana, Ricardo "Situation as Satirical Method." Norton Critical Editions: Jonathan Swift Gulliver's Travels. Ed. Robert A Greenberg. New York: W. W. Norton and Company Inc., 1961.

<li>Van Doren, Carl. Swift .New York: The Viking Press, 1930.

</ul>

# Essay: Book Four of Swift's Gulliver's Travels: Satirical, Utopian, or Both?

by Elsje Fourie
November 25, 2000

> Once kick the world, and the world and you will live together at a
> reasonably good understanding.

> Jonathan Swift

When Gulliver's Travels was first published in 1726, Swift instantly became history's most famous misanthrope. Thackeray was not alone in his outrage when he denounced it as "past all sense of manliness and shame; filthy in word, filthy in thought, furious, raging, obscene" (quoted in Hogan, 1979: 648). Since then, few literary works have been so dissected, discussed and disagreed apon. It is the magnum opus of one of the English language's greatest satirists, but certainly does not offer any easy answers. It is written like the typical travel book of the day, but instead of offering a relaxing escape from the real world, it brings us face to face with reality in all its complexity.

Of the four books comprising the work, by far the most controversial has been the last: "A Voyage to the Houyhnhnms". In it, the narrator, Gulliver, is deposited by mutineers on an island inhabited by two species. The Yahoos are dirty, savage and barbaric, with no capacity for reason. These wretched creatures physically resemble humans but immediately fill Gulliver with loathing. The Houyhnhnms, on the other hand, are a race of talking horses governed completely by reason. They lead natural, simple lives, and use the Yahoos for menial labour. They are so honest they cannot conceive of the notion of dishonesty. They regard Gulliver as a precocious Yahoo and, after a few years, banish him from the Island. Gulliver is heartbroken, having developed a love for these serene creatures and their way of life. He spends the rest of his life in England, trying talk to horses and regarding his fellow humans "only with Hatred, Disgust and Contempt".

Until the 20th century, criticism of book four tended to equate Gulliver with Swift. Gulliver would rather jump from the ship that "rescued" him than re-enter human society He cannot bear to look at his own reflection because of the resemblance he bears to the Yahoos. He sees himself as unworthy even to kiss the hoof of his Houyhnhnm master. This deeply offended an England which regarded man as the apex of creation and the paradigm of reason. Swift seemed to be damning mankind to a useless, horrible existence, without the prospect of any self-improvement or progress.

Modern criticism, however, can be divided into two broad schools of thought concerning the extent Swift wished to present the Houyhnhnm society as ideal.

James L. Clifford distinguishes between a 'soft' and a 'hard' approach (Lock, 1999). The approach one takes has a bearing on one's entire notion of the book: on the narrative technique, on the genre, and, most importantly, on the target of Swift's satire.

The soft approach, currently the more popular of the two, defends Swift from his 18th century detractors by refuting the idea of Swift as a people-hater. Exponents believe that there is a clear distinction between Gulliver and Swift, and that Swift is satirising his narrator rather than speaking through him. The Houyhnhnms are ironic devices not meant to be taken as ideal. Similarly, the reader is not to despise the Yahoos as Gulliver does, because the Yahoos, too, are abstractions. Gulliver's behaviour at the end is so absurd and silly that all the "insight" he has gained cannot be taken seriously. He regards the kind Captain Mendez as just another Yahoo, thus he is clearly unreliable, say the critics.

Furthermore, the Houyhnhm society is, by modern standards, far from ideal. Houyhnhnms love all members of their race equally, yet feel no romantic or sexual love. As supremely rational creatures, they see it as folly to mourn the death of a particular family member or friend. They reject anything that they are not familiar with. They exploit the Yahoos and procreate according to strict eugenic principles so as to breed an inferior servant class. Their language is limited and their culture primitive. They come across as remote, cold and dreary. George Orwell takes particular exception to the Houyhnhnms, calling them walking corpses. He sees their society as the epitome of totalitarianism, where the attitude is "we know everything already, so why should dissident opinions be tolerated?" (Orwell, 1971: 353).

Surely this could not have been Swift's idea of an ideal society, says the soft school. The Houyhnhnms must be symbols for man's rational element, and the Yahoos symbols for man's appetitive, sensual qualities. Swift hated deistic rationalism, popular in the 18th century, which relied on reason as the only guide for belief and action. Thus Gulliver is satirised for failing to find a balance between his humanity and his intellect. Crane sums up the imputed moral: "human nature is bad enough, but it is not altogether hopeless; reason is a good thing, but a life of pure reason is no desirable end for man". This critical approach tends to see Gulliver's Travels as a novel. Gulliver is a psychologically complex character and Swift uses him as a dramatic device.

This paper wishes to reject the easy compromises of this approach in favour of the traditional, 'hard' school of thought. Gulliver's Travel's is a satire, and Gulliver as satirical device does not have a fully-fledged personality. Although it is dangerous to equate narrator with author completely, Gulliver and Swift share the same basic view of human nature. The difference, as R. Crane says, is simply "between a person who has just discovered a deeply disturbing truth about man and is considerably upset and one who has known this truth all along and can therefore write of his hero's discovery calmly and with humour". There are no indications anywhere that Swift did not himself believe the words he puts into his hero's mouth. Readers have no other source but Gulliver, no contradicting views between which to decide. The ending of the book is not comical, but poignant. Gulliver, once so self-assured and proud of his species, has undergone a tragic disillusionment which cleverly forms the climax of the entire work.

The view that Gulliver's Travels does in fact despair of the human condition ties in with what is known of the author. His declaration that "Principally [he] hate[s] and detest[s] that animal called man" (quoted in Columbia, 1993) is certainly unequivocal enough. Swift was an orthodox Christian and a conservative. His puritanical views caused him to regard man as "fallen", as inherently sinful and evil. The Houyhnhnms represent prelapsarian existence. Unlike them, Adam and Eve were not content to live in blissful ignorance and brought about man's wretched state by following their appetites rather than their reason. Similarly, Gulliver's curiosity and thirst for adventure is the cause of all his troubles and of his cruelty to those he leaves behind.

He was certainly no democrat  he hated lords and politicians but felt no better about the lower classes. To claim Swift could not have sanctioned the exploitation of the Yahoos or lower caste of Houyhnhnms is to assume that Swift had modern values such as freedom and equality. These values resemble meliorism, which argued for the possibility of progress and improvement of society and which Swift dismissed even in his own day.

We also know, from another work, the Battle of the Books and from book three's Voyage to Glubdubbdrib that Swift had great respect for Classical Man. Although the Ancient Greeks and Romans were still human, they were as noble, uncorrupted and sensible as man could get. The Houyhnhnm society reminds of the Classical society in its simplicity. It corresponds particularly well with Plato's description of his ideal state in the Republic. In the Republic, everyone knows their place and duties in society. Inferiors do not strive to be equal to their superiors, and superiors do not ill-treat their inferiors. Children are educated only in mythology and physical fitness. The rulers have no private property or families, having given their children to the "community" at birth. Plato felt that only a few people possessed the capacity to reason properly, but that this capacity was the most valuable. He also distrusted the written medium, which he regarded as imperfect and misleading.

It seems as if Swift had Plato specifically in mind when creating the Houyhnhnms. Plato did not believe that his ideal society would ever come into existence, and Swift probably believed so even less. But unlike the soft school, which says that a life of reason is unattainable and undesirable, Swift believed that it is only unattainable. Whether Swift portrays the Houyhnhnm society as perfect for humans is an almost superfluous question, as it will never come about. Rather, it is a foil for human society, a device to show that we are not as rational as we think. Swift, in a letter to Pope, says that Gulliver's Travels aims at "proving the falsity of that definition animale rationale; and to show that it should be only rationis capax" (quoted in Hogan, 1979: 648). By this he means that man has the capacity for a smattering of reason, but that instead of using it to uplift himself, he uses it to increase his depravity. The singularly human phenomenon of war, for instance, so ridiculous when explained by Gulliver, requires some intelligence on the part of humans  but not much. Gulliver's sleeping quarters are literally halfway between the Yahoos and the Houyhnhnms, and this becomes a metaphor for man's paradoxical state. Swift includes sympathetic characters like Captain Mendez in the book to drive home the point that he is referring to all humans, including the reader who may imagine himself exempted.

Perhaps this is the reason why readers are so eager to soften the message of Gulliver's Travels  because they want to deflect the harsh glare of his satire away from themselves. This is certainly why the work has become a popular children's story. The idea that we are all Yahoos for life alarms people as much today as it did almost three centuries ago. Then there are the numerous references to excrement, which becomes a symbol for man's filthiness. When the Yahoos first see Gulliver, they defecate on his head, whereas Swift's ideal being, the horse, has particularly inoffensive dung and lives cleanly. This ties in with the contrast between the Yahoo diet and the Houyhnhnm diet. Gulliver cannot live on the monotonous but healthy diet of the Houyhnhnms, and this is further proof of barbarism.

However, Swift does, ultimately, give us a glimmer of hope for humanity. After all, this is the Irish patriot who pronounced Ireland "the most miserable country apon earth". Although he is passionate in his hatred for humankind, he is almost equally passionate in his love for it. True, this is no gentle humanist who sees the world basking in a rosy glow. Yet no-one who really does not care for his own species is so angry at finding it deficient. If Swift were really an all-out misanthrope, he would not have seen the point of trying to make humanity aware of its condition. He would not have given two thirds of his earnings to the poor. In his own forceful way, Swift dedicated his life to improving society. He knew he could not make Houyhnhnms of humans, but at least he could hold up his famous mirror of satire to show his fellow Yahoos what they really are.

## Bibliography

The Deists. 1991. The Concise Columbia Encyclopaedia. Columbia: Columbia University Press.

Rationalism. 1992. The American Heritage Dictionary of the English Language, 3rd ed. New York: Houghton Mifflin.

Jonathan Swift. 1993. The Columbia Dictionary of Quotations. Columbia: Columbia University Press.

Bennett, S. 2000. The Act of Reading Gulliver's Travels. In Readerly/Writerly Texts, edited by O. Oviedo, www.enmu.edu/Readerly/Writerly/4gullive.htm

Botha, W.M. & Du Toit, P.H. 1994. Guidelines for the Preparation of Written Assignments. 2nd ed. Pretoria: University of Pretoria.

Crane, R.S. 1971. <i>The Houyhnhnms, the Yahoos and the History of Ideas</i> In Penguin Critical Anthologies: Jonathan Swift, edited by D. Donoghue. Middlesex: Penguin Books, p. 363-385

Hogan, R. 1979. Jonathan Swift. The Macmillan Dictionary of Irish Literature. London: Macmillan Press, p. 636-637, 646-650.

Lock, F. 1999. Notes. Queens University, qsilver.queensu.ca/~lockfp/donoghue.html.

Orwell, G. 1971. <i>Politics vs. Literature: An Examination of Gulliver's Travels.</i> In Penguin Critical Anthologies: Jonathan Swift, edited by D. Donoghue. Middlesex: Penguin Books, p. 342-360.

Swift, J. 1940. Gullivers Travels. London: J.M. Dent and Sons.

Essay: Book Four of Swift's Gulliver's Travels: Satirical, Utopian, or Both?

# Quiz 1

1. **How tall are the Lilliputians?**
   A. About a foot tall
   B. Human size
   C. 5 to 6 inches
   D. Giant

2. **How tall are the Brobdingnags?**
   A. About a foot tall
   B. Human size
   C. 5 to 6 inches
   D. Giant

3. **What washes up on the shore of Lilliput?**
   A. Gulliver's hat
   B. Gulliver's gunpowder pouch
   C. Gulliver's boat
   D. Gulliver's glasses

4. **How does Gulliver put out the fire in the Empress's bed chamber?**
   A. With thimbles of water
   B. He doesn't
   C. He urinates on it
   D. With a hose

5. **What is Gulliver's role on his first voyage?**
   A. Captain
   B. Sailors
   C. Surgeon
   D. Passenger

6. **Which of the following is not one of the reasons Gulliver is convicted of treason in Lilliput?**
   A. He ate too much, causing a famine
   B. He encouraged the Blefuscudians in their peace proposals
   C. He refused to continue fighting for Lilliput
   D. He urinated on the Empress's bed chamber

7. **Who is Gulliver's enemy in Lilliput?**
    A. Flimnap
    B. Redresal
    C. Himnaptude
    D. Frank

8. **How does Gulliver arrive on Lilliput?**
    A. He can't remember
    B. He is dropped off there by a bird
    C. He and his crew land there
    D. He swims ashore after a shipwreck

9. **How do the Lilliputians decide who will take a high position in the court?**
    A. A tight-rope jumping contest
    B. Thumb wrestling
    C. Foot races
    D. Elections are held

10. **What is Gulliver's sentence after he is found guilty of treason in Lilliput?**
    A. Tickling
    B. Solitary confinement
    C. Having his eyes put out
    D. Execution

11. **Who are the enemies of the Lilliputians?**
    A. The Laputians
    B. The Brobdingnags
    C. The Blefuscudians
    D. Human beings

12. **Why did the Lilliputians divide?**
    A. They couldn't decide who should be emperor
    B. They cut their eggs at different ends
    C. They couldn't decide what to do with Gulliver
    D. They wore different sized heels on their shoes

13. **When Gulliver awakens on the shore of Lilliput, what is his condition?**
    A. Well-rested and comfortable
    B. Lying on his back tied up by hundreds of ropes
    C. Healthy but without any memory
    D. Having a terrible headache from having too much drink

14. **What did Flimnap say about Gulliver in order to slander him?**
    A. That Gulliver hid the queen's brush
    B. That Gulliver was a god
    C. That Gulliver was conspiring with the enemy
    D. That Gulliver slept with his wife

15. **How did Gulliver scare the people of Lilliput?**
    A. He clapped his hands loudly
    B. He sneezed
    C. He fired his pistol
    D. He stomped his foot

16. **How does Gulliver get home from Blefuscu?**
    A. He finds a boat floating off shore and repairs it
    B. He is picked up by a large bird
    C. He swims
    D. He doesn't

17. **How does Gulliver learn to speak the Lilliputian language?**
    A. A young girl teaches him
    B. Six scholars are employed to teach him
    C. He reads their newspapers
    D. He reads their books

18. **Who wrote Gulliver's Travels?**
    A. Alexander Pope
    B. Jonathan Swift
    C. Henry Fielding
    D. Lemuel Gulliver

19. **Why does Gulliver flee to Blefuscu?**
    A. The Lilliputians are going to execute him
    B. The Lilliputians are going to starve him to death
    C. The Lilliputians won't grant him his freedom
    D. The Lilliputians are going to put his eyes out

20. **How does Gulliver gain his liberty in Lilliput?**
    A. He tricks the Lilliputians
    B. He breaks free
    C. With his gentleness and good behavior
    D. He never gains his liberty

21. **Which of the Lilliputians is the nicest to Gulliver?**
    A. Flimnap
    B. Redresal
    C. The Emperor
    D. The Empress

22. **How do the Lilliputians hurt Gulliver when they first find him?**
    A. They shoot tiny arrows at him
    B. They let their animals bite him
    C. They hit him with stones
    D. They pull his hair

23. **What is the punishment for the Lilliputians who bother Gulliver?**
    A. They are put in prison
    B. They are given into Gulliver's hands
    C. They are forced to walk the tight-rope
    D. Death

24. **How does Gulliver's time in Lilliput end?**
    A. He stays until he dies at the age of 83
    B. He is given a grand boat filled with supplies
    C. He is convicted of treason
    D. He is carried away by a whale

## 25. Who raises the Lilliputian children?

A. Their parents

B. Animals

C. The government

D. Gulliver raises them while he's there

# Quiz 1 Answer Key

1. **(C)** 5 to 6 inches
2. **(D)** Giant
3. **(A)** Gulliver's hat
4. **(C)** He urinates on it
5. **(C)** Surgeon
6. **(A)** He ate too much, causing a famine
7. **(A)** Flimnap
8. **(D)** He swims ashore after a shipwreck
9. **(A)** A tight-rope jumping contest
10. **(C)** Having his eyes put out
11. **(C)** The Blefuscudians
12. **(B)** They cut their eggs at different ends
13. **(B)** Lying on his back tied up by hundreds of ropes
14. **(D)** That Gulliver slept with his wife
15. **(C)** He fired his pistol
16. **(A)** He finds a boat floating off shore and repairs it
17. **(B)** Six scholars are employed to teach him
18. **(B)** Jonathan Swift
19. **(D)** The Lilliputians are going to put his eyes out
20. **(C)** With his gentleness and good behavior
21. **(B)** Redresal
22. **(A)** They shoot tiny arrows at him
23. **(B)** They are given into Gulliver's hands
24. **(C)** He is convicted of treason
25. **(C)** The government

# Quiz 2

1. **What does Gulliver kill on his first night in Brobdingnag?**
   A. A beetle
   B. A cat
   C. A rat
   D. A butterfly

2. **What does Gulliver call his caretaker in Brobdingnag?**
   A. Grumdalclitch
   B. Grildrig
   C. Ardipcluft
   D. Lorbrulgrud

3. **How does Gulliver end up in Brobdingnag?**
   A. He swims ashore
   B. He can't remember
   C. He is left behind by his shipmates
   D. He follows a map to find the island

4. **Who is Gulliver's biggest enemy in Brobdingnag?**
   A. The farmer's workers
   B. Glumdalclitch
   C. The Queen's dwarf
   D. The farmer

5. **What does the King think Gulliver is at first?**
   A. A work of magic
   B. Artwork
   C. A mechanical creature
   D. A squirrel

6. **How does the Queen get Gulliver?**
   A. Gulliver asks for santuary in the palace
   B. She buys him from the farmer
   C. She finds him in the marketplace
   D. She has her dwarf steal him

7. **Who stays with Gulliver at the palace?**
   A. Glumdalclitch
   B. The farmer's wife
   C. The farmer
   D. Frumighty

8. **How does Gulliver travel in Brobdingnag?**
   A. In a specially made box
   B. In a wheelbarrow
   C. Sitting in the Queen's lap
   D. In a shoebox carried by a cat

9. **Why does the Queen's dwarf hate Gulliver?**
   A. He actually likes Gulliver
   B. He's afraid of Gulliver
   C. He's jealous of Gulliver
   D. Gulliver punched him in the nose

10. **What English invention does Gulliver tell the King about?**
    A. The plow
    B. The butterchurn
    C. Gunpowder
    D. Fire

11. **What does Gulliver make from the King's beard?**
    A. A broom
    B. A hat
    C. A comb
    D. A rope

12. **What does Gulliver make from the Queen's hair?**
    A. A brush and a chair
    B. A chair and a purse
    C. A stuffed bear and a brush
    D. A purse and a stuffed bear

### 13. How long is Gulliver in Brobdingnag?
A. About ten years
B. About two years
C. About five years
D. About fifteen years

### 14. How does Gulliver get off of Brobdingnag?
A. He makes a boat
B. He finds a boat
C. He is carried away by an eagle
D. He swims

### 15. What will happen to Gulliver if he talks about gunpowder again?
A. He will be exiled
B. He will be rewarded
C. He will be executed
D. He will be put in jail

### 16. Who finds Gulliver's traveling box?
A. Yahoos
B. The army
C. Sailors
D. The navy

### 17. Why doesn't Gulliver like Brobdingnagian music?
A. It is too low-pitched
B. It is too high-pitched
C. It has an awkward rhythm
D. It is too loud

### 18. What brings Gulliver to the top of the roof in Brobdingnag?
A. A monkey
B. A giraffe
C. A squirrel
D. A bird

19. **Why won't Gulliver sit on the chair he's made?**
    A. It is too small
    B. The queen won't let him
    C. He would disgrace the queen by sitting on her hair
    D. He doesn't want to offend the king

20. **Why is it difficult to adjust to life back in England after being in Brobdingnag?**
    A. He feels mentally inferior
    B. He is disgusted by their use of gunpowder
    C. He feels like a giant
    D. He feels like a Lilliputian

21. **What do Gulliver and the King discuss most often?**
    A. Algebra
    B. Zoology
    C. Astronomy
    D. Government

22. **Why do Gulliver's shipmates leave him behind in Brobdingnag?**
    A. They're chasing a whale
    B. They have to go find food
    C. They hate Gulliver
    D. They're being chased by a Brobdingnagian

23. **How long is Gulliver at home between his second and third voyages?**
    A. Two months and ten days
    B. Ten months and two days
    C. Two years and ten months
    D. Ten years and two months

24. **What is Gulliver's post on this third voyage?**
    A. Stoker
    B. Captain
    C. Surgeon
    D. Passenger

## 25. What disrupts Gulliver's third voyage?

A. The ship sinks
B. The ship crashes on a deserted island
C. The ship is attacked by pirates
D. The ship capsizes

# Quiz 2 Answer Key

1. **(C)** A rat
2. **(A)** Grumdalclitch
3. **(C)** He is left behind by his shipmates
4. **(C)** The Queen's dwarf
5. **(C)** A mechanical creature
6. **(B)** She buys him from the farmer
7. **(A)** Glumdalclitch
8. **(A)** In a specially made box
9. **(C)** He's jealous of Gulliver
10. **(C)** Gunpowder
11. **(C)** A comb
12. **(B)** A chair and a purse
13. **(B)** About two years
14. **(C)** He is carried away by an eagle
15. **(C)** He will be executed
16. **(C)** Sailors
17. **(D)** It is too loud
18. **(A)** A monkey
19. **(C)** He would disgrace the queen by sitting on her hair
20. **(C)** He feels like a giant
21. **(D)** Government
22. **(D)** They're being chased by a Brobdingnagian
23. **(A)** Two months and ten days
24. **(C)** Surgeon
25. **(C)** The ship is attacked by pirates

# Quiz 3

1. **Why is Gulliver punished by the pirates?**
   A. He doesn't speak the language
   B. He kills their captain
   C. He insults their captain
   D. He is too tall

2. **What punishment is given to Gulliver by the pirates?**
   A. He is forced to walk the plank
   B. He is punched in the face by the captain
   C. His left thumb is severed
   D. He is sent adrift in a canoe

3. **Where does Gulliver land after the pirate attack?**
   A. Laputa
   B. Lilliput
   C. Balnibarbi
   D. Brobdingnag

4. **What kinds of symbols do the Laputans wear on their clothes?**
   A. Religious and agricultural
   B. Agricultural and mathematical
   C. Mathematical and musical
   D. Astronomical and musical

5. **What is different about the bodies of the Laputans?**
   A. They can't stand for more than an hour
   B. Their heads slant to the left or right
   C. They have four legs
   D. They have no fingers

6. **What does Gulliver notice about the women of Laputa?**
   A. Nothing out of the ordinary
   B. They stand primarily on their hands
   C. They are very sexual creatures
   D. They are very well dressed

7. **Why don't the men of Laputa notice that their wives are cheating on them?**
    A. They don't love their wives anyway
    B. They are distracted by government
    C. They have poor eyesight
    D. They are too wrapped up in mathematics

8. **Who do the Laputan women prefer to their own husbands?**
    A. The Brobdingnagians
    B. The Balnibarbi
    C. Gulliver
    D. The Lilliputians

9. **Why does Gulliver ask to leave Laputa?**
    A. He is too smart for them
    B. He is bored
    C. He doesn't like the way they dress
    D. He is being treated poorly

10. **With whom does Gulliver stay in Balnibarbi?**
    A. Munodi
    B. Flimnap
    C. Glumdalclitch
    D. Rusalkirk

11. **How does Gulliver describe Munodi's home?**
    A. A mound of dirt
    B. Beautiful and well-kept
    C. Small
    D. In disrepair

12. **How does Gulliver describe the country on Balnibarbi?**
    A. Barren
    B. Hot
    C. Wet
    D. Lush

13. **How are towns in Balnibarbi punished?**
   A. They are charged a tax
   B. They are forced to walk a tight-rope
   C. They are never punished
   D. Laputa is moved above them

14. **Which of the following is not one of the experiments being tried by professors at the academy?**
   A. Turning excrement back into the food it began as
   B. Harnessing wind to make power
   C. Extracting sunlight from cucumbers
   D. Making gunpowder from ice

15. **What are the Laputians' talking sticks called?**
   A. Sinkers
   B. Flappers
   C. Gumpfuds
   D. Blumptufts

16. **How do the professors hope to catch traitors?**
   A. By asking them
   B. By examining their excrement
   C. By looking under their tongues
   D. By checking the color of their nose hair

17. **What is special about the Glubbdubdribians?**
   A. They are giant
   B. They are excellent mathematicians
   C. They can bring back the dead
   D. They are tiny

18. **What does Glubbdubdrib translate to?**
   A. Island of acrobatics
   B. Island of giants
   C. Island of firefighters
   D. Island of magicians

### 19. Which dead person does Gulliver talk to first?
A. Homer
B. Jesus
C. Alexander the Great
D. Caesar

### 20. Which of these deceased people does Gulliver NOT speak to?
A. King Charlemagne
B. Descartes
C. Aristotle
D. Alexander the Great

### 21. Why is Gulliver disturbed after he brings back dead English Yeomen?
A. They are sickly
B. They are missing limbs
C. They are heartier than the English of his time
D. They are insulting

### 22. When Gulliver goes to Luggnagg what does he disguise himself as?
A. A horse
B. A Lilliputian
C. A Dutchman
D. A sorcerer

### 23. In order to see the King of Luggnagg what must one do?
A. Dance for thirteen minutes
B. Lick the floor
C. Cry real tears
D. Balance on one foot

### 24. What does the King of Luggnagg do to courtiers he doesn't like?
A. Poisons the floor they have to lick
B. Feeds them to Brobdingnagians
C. Puts them in prison
D. Exiles them to Brobdingnag

25. **What is a Struldbrug?**
    A. A Luggnaggian magician
    B. An immortal Luggnaggian
    C. A Luggnaggian who mops the floor
    D. A young Luggnaggian

# Quiz 3 Answer Key

1. **(C)** He insults their captain
2. **(D)** He is sent adrift in a canoe
3. **(C)** Balnibarbi
4. **(C)** Mathematical and musical
5. **(B)** Their heads slant to the left or right
6. **(C)** They are very sexual creatures
7. **(D)** They are too wrapped up in mathematics
8. **(B)** The Balnibarbi
9. **(B)** He is bored
10. **(A)** Munodi
11. **(B)** Beautiful and well-kept
12. **(A)** Barren
13. **(D)** Laputa is moved above them
14. **(B)** Harnessing wind to make power
15. **(B)** Flappers
16. **(B)** By examining their excrement
17. **(C)** They can bring back the dead
18. **(D)** Island of magicians
19. **(C)** Alexander the Great
20. **(A)** King Charlemagne
21. **(C)** They are heartier than the English of his time
22. **(C)** A Dutchman
23. **(B)** Lick the floor
24. **(A)** Poisons the floor they have to lick
25. **(B)** An immortal Luggnaggian

# Quiz 4

1. **Where does Gulliver stop on his way from Luggnagg to England?**
   A. Japan and Ireland
   B. Spain and Ireland
   C. Japan and Amsterdam
   D. Amsterdam and Spain

2. **What is Gulliver's post during his final voyage?**
   A. Captain
   B. Oarsman
   C. Steward
   D. Surgeon

3. **What happens on Gulliver's fourth voyage?**
   A. Mutiny
   B. The crew is lost at sea
   C. War
   D. The ship capsizes

4. **How does Gulliver get to the land of the Houyhnhnms?**
   A. He is carried there by a giant eagle
   B. He is magically transported
   C. He swims ashore
   D. His crew drops him off on their island

5. **What are the humans called in the land of the Houyhnhnms?**
   A. Yahoos
   B. Googles
   C. Dingbats
   D. Flimnaps

6. **Who does Gulliver say are the stupidest Yahoos?**
   A. Sailors
   B. Doctors
   C. Lawyers
   D. Professors

7. **What concept do Houyhnhnms not understand?**
   A. Dignity
   B. Bravery
   C. Lying
   D. Honor

8. **What color is Gulliver's master?**
   A. Red
   B. Grey
   C. Black
   D. White

9. **Who does Gulliver think are the most virtuous?**
   A. Yahoos
   B. Brobdingnags
   C. Lilliputians
   D. Houyhnhnms

10. **How does Gulliver's Houyhnhnm master honor him?**
    A. By ignoring him
    B. By sneezing on him
    C. By asking him to sit farther away
    D. By walking around him three times

11. **What happens to Gulliver when he tries to bathe in the pond?**
    A. A Yahoo female tries to assault him
    B. He is captured by elves
    C. He nearly drowns
    D. He is captured by Brobdingnags

12. **What do the Houyhnhnms discuss during their Great Assembly?**
    A. Whether or not to execute Gulliver
    B. Whether or not to execute the Yahoos
    C. What do do with the Lilliputians
    D. Whether or not Gulliver is a Yahoo

13. **How do the Houyhnhnms keep track of their history?**
    A. They have no need for history
    B. They carve pictures in stone
    C. Through oral tradition
    D. They write it down

14. **How old does the average Houyhnhnm live to be?**
    A. 20-25 years old
    B. 40-45 years old
    C. 60-65 years old
    D. 70-75 years old

15. **Why is Gulliver asked to leave the island of the Houyhnhnms?**
    A. They are afraid he will die if he doesn't eat meat
    B. They are afraid he'll lead the Yahoos in a revolt
    C. Actually Gulliver wants to leave
    D. He is disrespectful of his master

16. **What does Gulliver do to his Houyhnhnm master before he leaves?**
    A. He slaps him across the nose
    B. He hugs his neck
    C. He kisses his hoof
    D. He strokes his mane

17. **What does Gulliver eat while living among the Houyhnhnms?**
    A. Salmon
    B. A kind of bread made from oats
    C. The stems of various flowers
    D. Corn meal

18. **What does Gulliver do when his master tells him it is time to leave the land of the Houyhnhnms?**
    A. Cheers
    B. Faints
    C. Drinks
    D. Cries

19. **Where does Gulliver want to live when he leaves the Houyhnhnms?**
   A. With the Lilliputians
   B. In England
   C. On a nearby island, alone
   D. In Portugal

20. **What is the name of the Portuguese captain?**
   A. Don Frederico
   B. Don Juan
   C. Don Pedro
   D. Don Javier

21. **What do the natives do to Gulliver?**
   A. Run away from him
   B. Shoot an arrow in his knee
   C. Welcome him warily
   D. Welcome him warmly

22. **What is Gulliver's reaction to the Portuguese sailors?**
   A. He thinks they're rude
   B. He can't believe how friendly they are
   C. He thinks they look like giants
   D. He finds them disgusting

23. **What does Gulliver do while on the Portuguese ship?**
   A. Helps the captain navigate
   B. Tells the crew about his journeys
   C. Stays in his cabin
   D. Works as a surgeon

24. **How many horses does Gulliver buy when he returns to England?**
   A. Twelve
   B. Ten
   C. Two
   D. Seven

25. **How many hours a day does Gulliver spend with his horses?**
    A. Twelve
    B. Two
    C. Four
    D. Seven

# Quiz 4 Answer Key

1. **(C)** Japan and Amsterdam
2. **(A)** Captain
3. **(A)** Mutiny
4. **(D)** His crew drops him off on their island
5. **(A)** Yahoos
6. **(C)** Lawyers
7. **(C)** Lying
8. **(B)** Grey
9. **(D)** Houyhnhnms
10. **(C)** By asking him to sit farther away
11. **(A)** A Yahoo female tries to assault him
12. **(B)** Whether or not to execute the Yahoos
13. **(C)** Through oral tradition
14. **(D)** 70-75 years old
15. **(B)** They are afraid he'll lead the Yahoos in a revolt
16. **(C)** He kisses his hoof
17. **(B)** A kind of bread made from oats
18. **(B)** Faints
19. **(C)** On a nearby island, alone
20. **(C)** Don Pedro
21. **(B)** Shoot an arrow in his knee
22. **(D)** He finds them disgusting
23. **(C)** Stays in his cabin
24. **(C)** Two
25. **(C)** Four

# ClassicNotes

# GradeSaver™

*Getting you the grade since 1999*™

## Other ClassicNotes from GradeSaver™

1984
Absalom, Absalom
Adam Bede
The Adventures of Augie
    March
The Adventures of
    Huckleberry Finn
The Adventures of Tom
    Sawyer
The Aeneid
Agamemnon
The Age of Innocence
Alice in Wonderland
All My Sons
All Quiet on the Western
    Front
All the King's Men
All the Pretty Horses
The Ambassadors
American Beauty
Angela's Ashes
Animal Farm
Anna Karenina
Antigone
Antony and Cleopatra
Aristotle's Ethics
Aristotle's Poetics
Aristotle's Politics
As I Lay Dying
As You Like It
Astrophil and Stella
The Awakening
Babbitt
The Bacchae
Bartleby the Scrivener
The Bean Trees

The Bell Jar
Beloved
Benito Cereno
Beowulf
Bhagavad-Gita
Billy Budd
Black Boy
Bleak House
Bluest Eye
The Bonfire of the
    Vanities
Brave New World
Breakfast at Tiffany's
Call of the Wild
Candide
The Canterbury Tales
Cat's Cradle
Catch-22
The Catcher in the Rye
The Caucasian Chalk
    Circle
The Cherry Orchard
The Chosen
A Christmas Carol
Chronicle of a Death
    Foretold
Civil Disobedience
Civilization and Its
    Discontents
A Clockwork Orange
The Color of Water
The Color Purple
Comedy of Errors
Communist Manifesto
A Confederacy of
    Dunces

Confessions
Connecticut Yankee in
    King Arthur's Court
The Consolation of
    Philosophy
Coriolanus
The Count of Monte
    Cristo
Crime and Punishment
The Crucible
Cry, the Beloved
    Country
The Crying of Lot 49
Cymbeline
Daisy Miller
Death in Venice
Death of a Salesman
The Death of Ivan Ilych
Democracy in America
Devil in a Blue Dress
Dharma Bums
The Diary of Anne Frank
Disgrace
Divine Comedy-I:
    Inferno
A Doll's House
Don Quixote Book I
Don Quixote Book II
Dr. Faustus
Dr. Jekyll and Mr. Hyde
Dracula
Dubliners
East of Eden
Emma
Ender's Game
Endgame

For our full list of over 250 Study Guides, Quizzes,
Sample College Application Essays, Literature Essays and E-texts, visit:

**www.gradesaver.com**

# ClassicNotes

# GrAdeSaver™

*Getting you the grade since 1999*™

# ClassicNotes

# GrⱯdeSaver™

*Getting you the grade since 1999*™

## Other ClassicNotes from GradeSaver™

My Antonia
Native Son
Night
No Exit
Notes from Underground
O Pioneers
The Odyssey
Oedipus Rex / Oedipus the King
Of Mice and Men
The Old Man and the Sea
On Liberty
On the Road
One Day in the Life of Ivan Denisovich
One Flew Over the Cuckoo's Nest
One Hundred Years of Solitude
Oroonoko
Othello
Our Town
Pale Fire
Paradise Lost
A Passage to India
The Pearl
The Picture of Dorian Gray
Poems of W.B. Yeats: The Rose
Portrait of the Artist as a Young Man
Pride and Prejudice
Prometheus Bound
Pudd'nhead Wilson
Pygmalion

Rabbit, Run
A Raisin in the Sun
The Real Life of Sebastian Knight
Red Badge of Courage
The Republic
Richard II
Richard III
The Rime of the Ancient Mariner
Robinson Crusoe
Roll of Thunder, Hear My Cry
Romeo and Juliet
A Room of One's Own
A Room With a View
Rosencrantz and Guildenstern Are Dead
Salome
The Scarlet Letter
The Scarlet Pimpernel
Secret Sharer
Sense and Sensibility
A Separate Peace
Shakespeare's Sonnets
Siddhartha
Silas Marner
Sir Gawain and the Green Knight
Sister Carrie
Six Characters in Search of an Author
Slaughterhouse Five
Snow Falling on Cedars
The Social Contract

Something Wicked This Way Comes
Song of Roland
Sons and Lovers
The Sorrows of Young Werther
The Sound and the Fury
Spring Awakening
The Stranger
A Streetcar Named Desire
The Sun Also Rises
Tale of Two Cities
The Taming of the Shrew
The Tempest
Tender is the Night
Tess of the D'Urbervilles
Their Eyes Were Watching God
Things Fall Apart
The Threepenny Opera
The Time Machine
Titus Andronicus
To Build a Fire
To Kill a Mockingbird
To the Lighthouse
Treasure Island
Troilus and Cressida
Turn of the Screw
Twelfth Night
Ulysses
Uncle Tom's Cabin
Utopia
A Very Old Man With Enormous Wings
The Visit

For our full list of over 250 Study Guides, Quizzes,
Sample College Application Essays, Literature Essays and E-texts, visit:

**www.gradesaver.com**

47615795R00063

Made in the USA
Middletown, DE
29 August 2017